THE GREAT BB GUN WAR OF '76

D.J. McWINNER

PROLOGUE

My Confession:

"What is wrong with you?" I have struggled to answer that frequently asked question. I have no short answer to the question and those who ask are never interested in a deep concise answer but it is a question I have pondered over the years.

This answer begins when dinosaurs ruled the earth. Until a colossal meteor disrupted the current order. Ice engulfed the planet then receded. The melting ice formed rivers that ate away at the land, digging up hidden minerals. Mammals adapted to their new role in the hierarchy. Amidst these transformations, a massive lake formed with no outlet. The giant lake carved benches into the sides of the mountains and the minerals deposited at the mouth of the mighty lake of no outlet.

As the colossal lake gradually diminished, humans spread across the land and eventually stumbled upon the rich mineral deposit, prompting extensive mining operations. Everything was fine until the 1970s happened, an era I experienced first hand while attending school in this mining town. From my fourth-grade classroom window, I could witness the scars left behind by the open-pit mine.

Trends sometimes don't make much sense outside of the zeitgeist and the 70s were a peculiar time, pre Star Wars but mid-disco. We drank freely and without worry from any garden hose. Concussions were still funny and on most street corners a public urinal could be found that we called 'phone-booths'. Everyman is a victim of the times he lives. Society at large recovered from the hangover of the 1960s with a more subdued theme. The trendy colors of the day were meant to depress us.

I was extraordinarily average. Average height, average size, average intelligence. Nothing special but I excelled mischief and fighting. As penance for my sins they isolated me and gave me math worksheets to work through to keep me busy. I worked away at long division but suffered at the imperfection of a problem with a remainder.

Once, a friend and I captured a wild pheasant, confining it within a pigeon coop. This free-spirited bird vehemently resisted being caged. Throughout my life, I often recalled that pheasant—especially during times when I felt confined to cramped desks with inadequate lighting. Nevertheless, I persevered, believing that hard work would eventually yield its rewards. Due to my unruly behavior, I was relegated to work on math packets instead of participating in the enticing arts and crafts class reserved for well-behaved students. Consequently, in college, I pursued engineering, based on the skills I had developed by that point.

Upon entering my first professional job after college, I found my workspace to be even smaller than the coop rejected by the wild pheasant. Reflecting upon the profound lesson the wise pheasant had attempted to teach me, I realized that I had been living my life incorrectly

I embarked on a journey of self-reinvention. First and foremost, I despised my middle name — a family name that my siblings and I used as an insult. In my quest for a new middle name, I began with a television cliché, "Danger," before adding "Jazz" as a tribute to a basketball team bearing the same name.

This is a slight embellishment of actual events.

Part 1

A colony of bees consists of 20,000-60,000 honeybees and one queen - the narrator of the film explained in a vaguely English accent. One of those grainy, worn films that seemed dated beyond its actual years and the projector clicked as the film wormed its way through the gears - *are highly evolved insects that engage in a variety of tasks. Communication, complex hive construction defense and division of labor are some of the characteristics bees have developed to exist successfully in social colonies.*

Often bees of different colonies compete for territory.

Mrs. Olsen entered the room, shut off the projector and announced: "The union called a strike, School is out." We sat in silence as we struggled to process this unprecedented and unexpected information. "Get out, O-U-T out," she reiterated.

EMPTY LOT

We met for battle on this piece of vacant ground called the Empty Lot, this abandoned parcel of land trapped between a failing farm and a boomtown called the River-bottoms. The name of the latter taken from an ancient, extinct river, now the site of middle-class semi-luxury homes as the Saxon copper mine company expanded operations. Middle managers who were willing to settle, longed for contemporary homes with a hint of country life.

But a curse gripped this land and tightened its hold on the realm. The great drought of '76 rendered barren the land in its wake with no concept of relief. Ambitious homebuilders bought the struggling farms for pennies on the dollar. The old life gave way for new, modern homes with burnt orange appliances and olive-green shag carpeting and popcorn ceilings.

Merle had a plan. That's what he did best. He made plans. We lived in the hills above the River-bottoms called Highland and now had to share our stomping grounds with invaders.

Merle enlisted a lowlander named Lance to help retake Empty Lot in the name of the Highlands. I found this Lance annoying. He reckoned himself funnier than me and his delusion only grew every time he got more laughs than me.

We thus resolved to seize Empty Lot with a furry of pinecones and barrage of dirt-clods. "Overtake 'em with the *element of surprise,"* Merle explained. "On the count of three," he said. "We'll charge 'em, in a blaze of glory style."

Not one of his best plans, clearly lifted from a scene from *Butch Cassidy and Sundance Kid.* We hastily inched our way through the thickets and got into position. "One," Merle whispered loudly. "Two." I put on my warrior face. Yet, I then sensed something, something slightly wrong. My subconscious attempted to tell me something though I couldn't quite put my finger on. Subtle at first and then suddenly it all snapped into focus. Something about my leg. My trousers felt warm and wet. I turned around to see Lance peeing on my leg. In the heat of the battle I made a tactical mistake. *Never turn your back on that kid.*

Honey Bees communicate by way of a figure-eight type dance called a waggle dance. Workers share information with other members of the colony about direction and distance to patches nectar and pollen.

I stormed from the bushes, stomped about and cursed. I tossed down my stock of pinecones and dirt-clods and stomped about dancing a tantrum. *I hate it when this kid gets one over on me.*

Shocked and confused by my display, the defending Lowlanders exited their hiding places to witness the fracas. Merle seized the opportunity and launched a major assault of pinecones on every Lowlander. Stunned but laughing, they surrendered.

"Something is seriously wrong with him," I mumbled as I walked home to fetch a clean pair of trousers.

"What are you doing?" my mother asked.

"Pants. Clean pants," I said.

"Oh, what is wrong with you boys?"

She wrinkled her face and thought for a second, "Oh, you should just tell him to stop doing that," she said in her nasally drone. That's the sort of banal advice you get from mothers in these matters.

"Ha, yeah, that'll fix him," I said.

"Well, you're not going back out. It's almost time for dinner."

THE 1970S

It was the worst of times, the 1970s and although I knew of no other age, I suspected these times were lacking as we filled the void with re-runs of *Star Trek*, set in the distant future and *Happy Days*, a show set in the recent past. People longed for anything different in this peculiar epoch. The fashions, politics; all wrong and tragic and also begun the era when white people forgot how to dance. Everyone just sort of gave up.

This scourge of nihility inflicted itself on food and that night's rations proved no exception. The unfortunate gastronomical experiment and for which we gave thanks came from a store bought can called *Chung King, Chow Mein*. Barely recognizable as a food, some sort of green-greyish sort of stew-like substance. Not a good color for food. Topped off with some dry noodles thus rendering the noodles uneatable as well. A school lunch like mystery now mocking me at home. "Eat. There are starving people in China". She then offered orange Jell-O as side dish, which is normally acceptable but she got creative and tried to sneak carrot peelings into the Jell-O, per local custom.
Jell-O isn't broken and does not need to be fixed I thought. Everything had to be tampered with but I had enough and that night I drew a line in the sand: "I'm not eating this," I announced. She ignored me. This violated so many food rules. Food should be in its most basic form and must never touch other food. It mixes in the stomach, not on the plate.

"Oh, just try it," she scolded. "You can't have pizza every meal don'tcha know."

"Pizza is the perfect food," I countered the argument with facts. "All four food groups."

"You're not leaving this table until you finish," she said definitively.

I had a few ways out of this Chinese food Mexican stand-off. My younger brother once tried to get out of eating food mistakes by putting his dinner in his milk. A brilliant plan because the milk color would hide most uneatable food, but this rookie mistake backfired when he couldn't leave the kitchen table until he finished his milk.

I had experimented with putting food I refused to eat in a drawer in the adjacent kitchen hutch. This plan only bought me time but I would have pay later when she found it. *No worry*, I had a new move. I would have to 'pocket it'. As I sat there ruminating of all the adventures taking place at Empty Lot without me, I anxiously stuffed every bit of the uneatable swill into both front pockets. I then passed the clean plate test and returned to outdoors for more adventures.

"Oh, be careful out. There's a prowler…." her voice trailed off as I ran out the door.

I had heard some unusual thefts had taken place lately. Nothing big, just random knickknacks went missing from people's homes without explanation. The sort of thing you don't notice until it's needed. No evidence of break-in and no one could figure out how they got in and out.

I stopped by Pinky's house at the bottom of Dead Man's Hill en route to Empty Lot. I rang the doorbell but no one answered. I cut thru his yard continuing on to Empty Lot. His large, deranged dog *Princess Barry* let out a growl, warning me to keep my distance. This insane, slightly inbred Doberman they kept chained in the yard, remained hostile to anyone outside of their family. *I hate that dog.*

The mad dog wore a radial path in the lawn marking the maximum length of her chain so we knew exactly how close we could get. I stood just past her line of death and emptied one pocket full of Chung King onto the ground on Doberman's side of the path. She stopped barking, sniffed the Chung King, licked it a bit and then walked away. Not even a crazy dog would eat that swill.

"All this land once belonged to us. The Roys settled this land," my old man used to tell me. My Aunt, the family historian told me the story of my great, great grandfather who settled here with his five wives. "Nothing grew in this dry unforgiving land," she explained. "But they worked the earth, bent it to their will, irrigated and diverted water from the mountains to valley below to grow crops and raise cattle. They survived and eventually even prospered. However, at some point, between the addition of wife #2 and wife #5, wife #1 grew annoyed and burned all of his belongings."

My father discounted this story explaining "When you're Scottish, at some point, someone with red hair will be setting fire to all your belongings."

I later learned a couple of the sons met their maker at the hands of a legendary gunslinger over a mule and like that, the family scattered throughout the old west. Everyone except us. We somehow managed to cling to this place resisting the best efforts of fate.

A grasshopper landed on my shirt interrupting my thoughts. *Because you never know when a grasshopper might come in handy* so I clasped it between my hands and put it in my still Chung King filled pocket.

There are many challenges on the short-cut to Empty Lot from Pinky's house. First, find the loose board in the fence in Pinky's yard. Just pull it forward and slip through the space. Next, a quick dash across the corner of Old Man Fisher's land. This was a risky shortcut because you had to sprint across a portion of his land to avoid his deranged ostrich. Old Man Fisher kept a lot of exotic animals on his land that he rotated around between crops.

I sprinted across the field catching the attention of the berserk ostrich. He charged and caught up to me as I reached the four-foot-high stone wall which bisected Old Man Fisher's land and the River-bottoms. Just a Fosbury flop with a shoulder roll on the other side then back on my feet.

Next stop, the hedge bushes marking the border to Fisher's land and the road. I pushed my way thru a secret weak spot in the bushes to get to the other side.

BARKIES

By the time I got to the Empty Lot Merle had worked out the details of the Lowlanders surrender with the smoking of a ceremonial barky.

Barkies, true barkies come the paper-thin bark of the Quaking Aspen that instantly rolls when pulled from the tree. A tightly rolled Quaking Aspen barky burned slowly, enjoyed by some locals as an occasional reward. Some philistines use the bark of the Rocky Mountain Sycamore but I find it banal, pedestrian with an uninspired aftertaste.

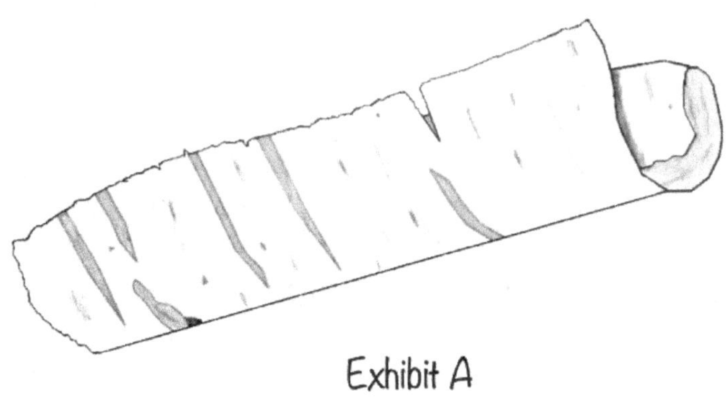

Exhibit A

Quaking Aspens thrived in the surrounding mountains above but are rare here in the arid valley below. We had to improvise and barkies thus became anything that could be burned. The Wild Milk Weed Thistle would work in a pinch or even the stock of a Trumpet flower for the truly desperate. Catch as catch can.

Merle took pride in his barky skills and strived to fashion bigger yet more lavish barkies. Merle once crated his greatest barky by rolling some dry straw in a paper plate. Loosely bound with an elastic band, he offered it up to Pinky. Merle lit the other end just as Pinky inhaled. The barky immediately combusted into flames like a roman candle. The fire instantly consumed the barky as Pinky inhaled a giant cloud of dark, smelly, blue-grey smoke singeing his eyebrows and bangs. He coughed, snorted and then puked. He vowed to never again smoke experimental barkies. He smelled of burned weeds and burnt hair. This is how he earned his nickname *Stinky*.

Everyone is gifted two nicknames; a good one, and a bad one. The former used for flattery, when we wanted something. The latter is used to control annoying habits. Eventually one name dominates over the other one, depending on behavior and therefor everyone earns their own name.

In the case of a Pinky, so called by his family because of his ginger hair and pink skin. This name quickly mutated to *Stinky* after the giant barky incident.

I arrived at the Empty Lot just as Lance took a hit from Merle's barky of peace. A blend of hay and dry leaves rolled in ruled paper. A classic. And Lance, showing off, sucked in way too much smoke. He doubled over and coughed uncontrollably as he tried to catch his breath. *Righteous justice is on my side.* I sidled up causally, removing from my pocket the Chung King fermented grasshopper that had been marinating in the warmth of my front pocket. I cupped it in the palm of one hand. I sneaked behind Lance and covered his mouth with my open palm, shoving it into his mouth. Instinctively he chewed for approximately 3.3 mississippis before realizing he had indeed been had.

He broke free of my grasp and spun around to see the culprit behind the escapade.

"Grasshopper," I said as he spat out the contents onto the ground and attempted to scrape the remains off his tongue with his fingertips. *It's like they say: revenge is a dish best served cold, with a Chung King and grasshopper.*

He stood, stunned while I did a victory lap, hands in the air, proud of getting over on someone. He countered by throwing wild haymakers. *Not the reaction I expected.* I stepped back to avoid his punches. I quickly made up a peace offering. "Right here," I said pointing to my left shoulder with my right pointer finger, "right here man." Figuring I could take one punch and it would be over. A slug on the shoulder would be a tacit agreement the score is even.

Confused by my offer, he stopped and looked about at everyone.

"This ain't over," he said and went home.

The next morning we met again at Empty Lot. "Did you bring it?" Merle asked. As part of the peace agreement with the Lowlanders it was agreed that the dumbest Lowlanders would swipe a nudie magazine from his older brother, so we could finally unravel this mystery of forbidden knowledge and get on with our lives.

"No," Cobra said. Cobra earned his name from his slight lisp and sometimes spat when he spoke. "He almost caught me. This is all I got." He produced a worn picture, torn from a magazine from his pocket. He showed us a black and white photo of a woman in a bikini.

"This does not square us," Merle said and walked away in disgust.

THE FORT

Bees are social insects who work together in a sort of collective called a hive.

Hives are normally built in an enclosed, dry space, in a tree trunk, roof or wall cavity or a man-made hive.

Now finally at peace with the Lowlanders we could proceed with the construction of the fort at Empty Lot.

Each kid brought their own ideas and skills to the project. We borrowed scraps of materials from nearby construction sites. We made it up as we went. Bits of 2x4's were nailed to trees. Chunks of plywood were nailed to the 2x4's and a patchwork fort began to take shape as we just made it up as we went. Inspired by kid optimism and country ingenuity.
We eventually abandoned plans for second and third floors over Spock's constant complaints about safety, but mostly because of a lack of building materials at that point.

Lance showed up one morning rolling a giant wooden wheel he found at a nearby construction site. The kind used to store a bundle of electrical cable. We put this wheel in the center of the fort on the dirt floor with rocks all around the wheel where we sat and planned our adventures.

Every evening we gathered around the giant wooden wheel at Empty Lot. There we made plans for adventures while Merle entertained with tricks. "Observe," he said after emptying all the powered from several caps for his cap gun. He then created a spark with two rocks and the powered combusted into a magnificent blue flame and disappeared in an instant, thus delighting the Lowlanders.

SPOCK HOLLIDAY

I met Spock Holliday in Kindergarten when he helped work through my first existential crisis. It started with the buffet of colors known as the Crayola 64. As I pondered *the point of the white crayon? You can't color white on white paper; it doesn't show up on colored paper.* Then it struck me.... "what color do we color white people?"

"Ah, simple," he said scanning over the 64-crayon empire. He produced the color *peach.* He handed me the peach colored crayon that looked a bit dill. I reached for the box to sharpen the crayon. "Stop, I'll sharpen my own crayons thank you," he said. "See, and if you trace the outline of the drawing with the crayon before coloring the inside you can avoid coloring outside the lines," he explained.

This Highlander with an Elvis haircut, he earned his name by being square and as an admirer of Spock, he embraced the name. But he also dressed in western garb. Square toed cowboy boots, because pointy toed boots are too proud and western shirts with the top button fastened. Nice, but not fancy. He looked 100 years out of place, like how a 1960s Hollywood imagined a character from the old west dressed.

CRAZY RAY

Grandma Moses, my older brother, earned his name from our old man. He had trouble focusing and often frosted our father with his constant distractions as he despised delays. "Come on Grandma Moses," the old man would shout when he became distracted by a caterpillar or a stick or a something shiny on the ground and would stop for closer examination.

Moses planned a caper in the River-Bottoms one night over an imagined slight by a new arrival. "At nightfall see," he explained "we'll sneak down and TP their house." I didn't need the details.

That night, dressed in black, armed with rolls of Charmin single ply, we snuck to the River-bottoms. We ran stealth. We sprinted serpentine, hiding in the shadows en-route. "Up there ahead," Moses said pointing to an alley between two houses, lined with wood fences on both sides. "Through there," he whispered, grabbing me by the shirt pulling me forward.

Halfway through the alley Moses suddenly stopped and following closely I crashed into him. "Hey man."

"Shh, Hear that?" He whispered. "Someone's coming."

I figured he just lost focus like he does, but then I heard it too, the sounds of footsteps coming our way. Fast footsteps echoing and getting closer. And then, up ahead I could make out the image of person sprinting our way.

Unsure what to do so we just stepped out of the way. With our backs up against the fence we made way for the charging stranger and as the figure passed us, he said to us casually, "You better run."

Then another personage appeared in the distance. Rather than take any chances we decided to flee. We ran and took refuge in a hiding place in Old Man Fisher's shrubs. From there we watched a very angry man walk up and down the street stalking his prey. I have a giggle reflex in tense situations. I let out a snicker. Moses put his hand over my mouth and held tight to stifle me. The angry man stopped. He stared at the bushes, unsure if he had heard something or not. Seconds felt like an eternity. He finally gave up and walked off.

I had trouble sleeping, fretting about fallout from our failed TP mission, but eventually dozed off thinking up alibis for the caper.

The next morning, I met Merle and the Lowlanders at Empty Lot. We had just begun our plans for the day when I heard that same voice from the night before.

"Hello," he said. I didn't have to look. I knew that voice. I just ignored him, pretending I didn't hear him, but he never relented. "I said *hello.*" I continued to ignore but the stress got to me and I looked over at Merle for support.

He never bothered Merle for fear of his older brothers. They called him *Lefty,* not for being left-handed, he was not. But because, legend had it, a sheep dog bit off his right testicle. The story seemed dubious to me, even at my young age when I believed anything, but Merle's oldest brother taught me the following philosophy: *If someone tells you a sheep dog bit off their nut, just take their word for it because why do you care if he's lying.*

"I said *Hello,*" he repeated loudly and more annoyed, daring me to continue ignoring him. Pinky started to back away from me and most the other kids inched toward their bikes to make quick get-away in the event that all this turned ugly.

Despite being the same age of Merle's oldest brother Crazy Ray spent much of time bullying local kids. Evil and dumb, I had never seen a ghost, UFO, or Bigfoot but, I dealt with this anomaly often as he seemed to have a lot of time on his hands.

"You didn't see anything," he said pointing his finger at me.

"What? I don't know what you're talking about."

He grabbed me by the shirt and pulled me in close. "I just looked in her window for like a second see, then her father saw me and he freaked out," He explained. "You're not gonna say a word about this, right?" he asked in a menacingly. "Right?"

"Okay," I said, trying to get out of this conversation as quickly as possible as I didn't want to have to explain his story to other kids there who would have follow-up questions.

"Fine," he said shoving me to the ground.

He looked about, sniffed, snorted up a loogie and spat at Granola's feet.

He spotted a baseball mitt on the handlebars of a lowlander's bike. Lefty removed the mitt from the bike. Examined it a bit. "Looks broke in real good," he said wearing it on one hand and striking out with the other fist. He pretended to hand it back but instead flung it frisbee style over the fence.

Then Pinky caught his eye. "You," he said. "Come here."

Pinky retreated two steps back and said "No?" like as if asking permission to refuse. Crazy Ray charged after him and Pinky turned and ran but Crazy Ray instantly chased him down like a rabid hyena after a gimpy gazelle. Crazy Ray put him his back and sat on his chest. "You made me come get you. That's gonna cost ya," Ray said viscerally like having an out of body experience. Someone shook the hell out of this snow-globe and released the monster onto the world.

Crazy Ray reached over and grabbed a handful of grass and plugged Pinky's nose. Pinky clenched his mouth shut and moved his head left to right. Crazy Ray had endless patience for this game, plugged his nose and waited for Pinky to open his mouth for air and as soon as he did Crazy Ray shoved a handful of grass into his mouth. "This family has a dog you know. This lawn is his bathroom," he whispered. "Now chew".

Pinky chewed with his mouth wide open trying to keep any grass juice from sliding down his gullet. He chewed to Crazy Ray's satisfaction and he let him go. Head down and ashamed Pinky headed home.

Crazy Ray hopped to his feet, grabbed Granola and put him on the ground. He commenced to punching him in the leg whilst singing: *The polka dot door, the polka dot door, what's behind the polka dot door* punching him in the thigh on each downbeat of the song. This ongoing punishment he inflicted on Granola for him watching this kid show years ago.

SCOUTING

"Are those milk cows?" Question Mark asked as we passed Old Man Fisher's place on our way to scouts.

I usually ignored this persistent kid but he knew he had a captive audience. This Lowlander earned his name by constantly talking and an inquisitive nature. *That kid would talk to a corpse* Merle used to say. He annoyed many by being interactive, always asking questions making it difficult to tune him out.

"I reckon he uses them for milk," I said.

"Right, but can you get milk from those cows?"

"Yes," I said. "Don't you see those things on its belly?" I asked putting both my hands on my stomach with both pointer and middle fingers extended imitating a cow's utter. "Like this," I said.

"I thought all cows have those?"

"All cows do have those."

He grew more frustrated and finally circled about to the point of his question. "Are those boy cows or girl cows?"

"Those are girl cows," I said. "That's what these things are," making the utters with my fingers again and moving my belly about to drive home the point.

"But those cows have horns," He said.

"Right, cows have horns."

"But I thought only boy cows have horns."

"What do you think these things are for then?" Again, making an utter with my fingers. Those are girl cow things".

He paused for a second. "Only an ignorant redneck would know that."

"Alright," I said thinking of the best way to settle his hash when our suddenly our conversation was interrupted when a flying apple hit Question Mark in the face.

"Hey man," he complained when another apple came flying towards us. And another, from the direction of Old Man Fisher's orchard. Crazy Ray grabbed another apple from the tree and threw it. I jumped out of the way to avoid the pitch. He was surprisingly accurate with his throws despite having a cigarette in his mouth.

"Better run pussies," he ordered. We sprinted the rest of the way to scouts to the sound of his boisterous laugh.

"Today we are going to paint our birdhouses," Spock Holiday's mother announced as she led us to a picnic table in the backyard patio. Spock Holiday's parents led our local scout troop and his mother, the den-mother took charge of the afternoon's activities.

"Here are the paints, brushes and stirrers," Spock's mother said setting them out on the picnic table. She took her seat at the end of the bench, closest to the phone where she could gossip with whomever would listen on the other end. "Oh, yeah another break-in I heard," she said with her nasally accent. "This time at the old Winter's place. And now a peeping-Tom"

"Oh, you don't say," I could make out the muffled voice on the line.

"And still no rain, if we don't get any soon there won't be any fruit this year," she chatted on.

Spock's mother, a robust woman, sat at one end of the bench required the rest of us acted as ballast, but as the attention span of ten-year-old boys tends to wane we vacated the bench one by one until only one kid remained and the bench which tipped like a teeter totter launching sole unfortunate kid on the far end into the air and rolling her onto the floor.

She struggled for a while to get up like a turtle on its back but she finally managed to roll over and get upright. She laughed it off. She had a good sense of humor about this sort of thing. "I suppose I should sit in the middle," she said.

She set out a variety of paint colors, brushes and stirrers for mixing the paint. I focused on my project and got lost in the moment when Lance interrupted me. "Here," he said handing me the business end of a stirrer. Instinctively I accepted the offering without thinking but few nanoseconds later I realized my hand felt moist and he hoodwinked me. I opened my hand to see my palm caked with sticky red paint.

I looked up at him. With a grin on his face he said "Right

here man," pointing to his left arm with his right pointer finger.
"Right here."

STAR TREK

Moses found out that a new Star Trek club had formed and would be meeting at the library. Excited by the prospects of getting our hands on this new tech we talked our mother into taking us. I knew the show was fiction but do to a misunderstanding I had from an episode of time travel, I failed to grasp how far in the future the show was set.

The reality of the club did not live up to they hype. We walked into the meeting room to see that we were the youngest ones there. They argued about the prime directive and how Dr Harry Rudd invented the mood ring.

The room of nerds discussed purging their emotions thru Vulcan rituals when finally, they announced we could meet in the back of the room to inspect the phasers, communicators and tricorders. I didn't understand how they got their hands on such otherworld gadgets but I didn't care as I just wanted to inspect the technology to see how it worked.

The first great disappoint of my life happened when I figured out these were just plastic models. The same ones Moses had put together months ago.

I took inventory of my life up to that point and decided I still wanted to get of this planet and therefor had some Star Trek left in me. I joined my local nerds at Spock's for the Star Trek game.

The game always started in the basement. They had an organ with sliding bars for volume, bass and treble. A few random notes on the organ then slide all three bars at the same time forward then back. Sprint to the imaginary spots in front of the fire place whilst imitating transporting sounds to transport to the planet below, in the back yard.

Spock played his part earnestly. "Captain," he said presenting me a stone he found. "There are some unique geological features on this planet," he said handing me the rock.

Spock interrupted himself when he noticed Lance, Question Mark and Cobra were there and had witnessed the entire exchange.

"Ha, nerds," Lance said noticing the wee paper triangles we had cut out and pinned to our shirts.

Damnit, not these guys I thought. Embarrassed and with the stone in my left hand I fired a warning shot. *This should do the trick.* A one in a million-luck shot hit Cobra square in the temple. Dazed, he fell off his bike. Everyone on my side ran off. Lance and Question Mark just stood there stunned by the turn of events. This Cobra earned his name from his *slight* lisp, spat a lot when speaking. Cobra stood taller than most kids his age and therefor unaccustomed to any sort of assault. This rock attack left too confused for any retaliation. He just wandered off rubbing his temple.

Cobra ruminated over The Rock Throwing incident of '76 and decided he wanted to beat me up "real good" Merle explained, but as an astute negotiator, he continued, "Good news, I talked him down to one punch in the gut. This will keep the parents out it". So, we scheduled a gut punching at Empty Lot for noon.

But once we returned to Empty Lot Cobra sought to change the deal. "I wanna hit him with a rock," he said. Lance and Merle talked it over and reached an agreement. "Rock Duel," they announced. "At twenty paces." The estimated distance of the first offense.

Pinky brought us a selection of rocks. Cobra made the challenge so I chose first. I strategized and selected the smoothest of the lot. Cobra picked the largest. We stood back to back and marched off twenty steps away from each other. I took aim and threw but missed my target inches. Cobra reacted and stepped aside.

"No fair," I complained. "He moved."

"Dodge again and you'll get blindfolded," Merle warned.

Cobra warmed up and I shut my eyes and counted down my fate. He put all his anger, all his shame and rage and put into his rock. He wound up and hucked a wild pitch which sailed pasted me wide right. *Cobra can't throw. Noted.*

"Rocks," Merle yelled. Pinky and Spock gathered up more stones and brought them over. Again, we made our choices. I took aim and launched a poor throw which soared far over his head. This time Cobra took time taking aim and threw a weak shot, sacrificing force for accuracy but the rock hit the ground in front of me and rolled close to my feet.

"Rocks," Merle yelled. Pinky brought us more stones.

I again took aim and threw a vicious uncontrolled pitch which sailed far right. Emboldened by his poor accuracy at this distance I figured he would never hit me. I decided to taunt. I arched my hips forward and made a strike zone around my groin area, angering him and enraged he threw another hard pitch which landed far into the trees behind me.

I let out a chuckle, proud that I annoyed him so.

Merle again shouted "Rocks" and Spock brought us the last of his reserves. Pinky started gathering more rocks as it seemed this competition would last a while.

I took my time aiming and this time threw and easy lob which fell far short landing near his feet as he faked interest watching it roll past his feet.

I again arched my hips forward, taunting him with a vulnerable target. I squinted my eyes shut to show my lack of fear. He tried to stay focused but is easily enraged and just as he launched another wide pitch Pinky yelled "Gold". I opened my eyes and saw this rock coming toward my presented target in slow motion. I panicked and reactively jumped left, out of the way unwittingly jumping into the path of the curve rock he pitched hitting me square in the target. Everyone had abandoned the rock throwing contest to investigate Pinky's claim. I dropped to the ground and rolled about on the earth writhing in pain. Distracted by Pinky's announcement, all had missed the direct shot. Cobra protested, "Hey, I hit him," but no one cared as they focused their attention on Pinky's gold.

I hobbled my way over to investigate Pinky's claim. He had a medium size throwing stone in his hand. This stone had jagged edges, looked metallic and reflected a gold light. *It would have made a good throwing stone.* Spock and Merle took turns studying it. "Fool's gold," Spock said.

"Right," Merle said "Gold."

"No. Fool's gold," he repeated.

"Right fool, Gold," Merle repeated louder and his showmanship overshadowing Spock's analysis.

Everyone spread out and investigated the area for more shiny rocks. Pinky started where he found the first stone found two more setting off a full fool's gold rush at Empty Lot.

By the next morning a full mining operation began at Empty Lot. We started the day early. Merle directed the digging twins where to work. These two brothers earned their name from their interest in hole digging. Pinky brought a wood box frame with a wire mesh screen inside. He dumped a shovel full or earth on the screen and shook it leaving only the rocks behind. He then shifted thru the remaining rocks, examining each one for gold content.

We toiled all with little success, only three more gold rocks were found in the vicinity of where Pinky found the first ones. Merle ordered all the other holes be filled and focused all our efforts at Pinky's claim. "Pinky, move your pile of rocks into the fort," Merle said and Pinky grabbed a bucket and moved them inside where they could be used later.

Merle brought a tin tool box his brother made in metal shop. He stored all the best fool's gold in the box and kept it in the fort for safe keeping.

FAKE FOOL'S GOLD

I got an early morning phone call from Merle. "Come over," he said. "I have a plan." I hopped on my bike right away and rode over to his house as his plans never disappointed. I could hear him working away in the garage. He had his father's tackle box on the work bench along with a hammer and a blow torch.

"Lookey here," he said showing me an old-fashioned skeleton key. "Traded Granola all the gold for it.

"All the gold?"

"Not to worry, I've got a plan to get more."

The fool's gold at Empty Lot became scarce as we had picked the area clean.

Merle had a bunch of lead fishing sinkers on the workbench. He grabbed a handful of the smaller sinkers, placed them on the anvil, struck a flame with a small handheld torch. "Stand back" he said. He adjusted the flame from a chaotic yellow to a focused thin blue flame and commenced to melting the sinkers, heating them into a molten pool of liquid metal. As it started too cool, he took a smooth stone, about the size of his palm and beat them into one rock like shape.

He dropped the hot led rocks into an old paint bucket full of water to cool them down. One they dried, he took a can of gold spray paint and covered them in gold.

Brilliant. "Back in a flash," I said and ran home to raid my old man's fishing gear. *Jackpot.* I grabbed as many sinkers as I could carry.

I rode back to Merle's house where we spent the rest of the morning working on our latest project and that's how Merle turned lead into fool's gold.

Back at Empty Lot we were again in business buying everything the lowlanders were willing to sell us.

The fool's gold at Empty Lot became scarce. Jealous of Merle's success Lance and Cobra grew suspicious. "How come you still find gold," Lance asked. "We've dug everywhere, and haven't found anymore."

"Pinky's claim," Merle replied.

"Okay, we're gonna dig there too."

"I can't allow that. It's Pinky's claim," Merle replied.

Merle ordered the Digger twins to cover Pinky's claim with a tarp. He then covered the tarp with a layer of dirt to blend in with the ground in a way he would know if it had been tampered with.

We left the fort and returned with our BB guns to protect the claim but when we returned all the lowlanders had taken over the fort and barricaded themselves inside.

Merle put his BB gun back over his shoulder and removed his pellet pistol for close range.

"Get out", he ordered.

Instead of submitting they returned a barrage of rock projectiles. A rare tactical error, Merle order we put the mined stones inside the fort for safe keeping along with the tool box treasure box and the cache of fake fool's gold.

"This ain't over", Merle said and we left.

We regrouped and Merle returned with the Highland army, all armed with BB guns and we surrounded the fort.

"Open up," Merle ordered. "We have a treaty." Merle tried to push against the board barricading the entrance but Lowlanders had fortified it.

Merle gave the signal and they opened fire, BB guns, shooting over the fort walls.

The guns pumping and making a small *whoosh* sounds with each fire. The Highland army stopped firing to reload and the lowlanders launched a rock assault.

"Rocks are against the treaty," Merle complained but they ignored and kept throwing.

The highland army pulled back out of range of the rocks but also put the fort out of range of the BB's.

We hatched a plan. At nightfall to break into fort and take back the tin tool box of treasure. I dressed in black, snuck out the basement window, I hid in the shadows and waited for Merle across from Pinky's house. The Crazy dog paced back and forth, watching me but remained quiet as I kept my distance.

"Did you have trouble sneaking out," I asked.

"Huh, sneak out? I just left. Hop on."

I got on the handlebars and we rode over to Empty Lot. The Lowlanders had barricaded the entrance from the inside. Merle tried to push his way through but couldn't get it to budge. "Those fools did a good job on this door," he said finally giving up. "We need to find another way in."

Merle switched on the flashlight and we walked around to the other side of the fort to find another way in found someone had already knocked down the wall.

"What's going on here?" Merle asked as we slowly made our way inside the fort.

Merle shined the light around. The fort had been sacked. The table overturned and on its side. We searched all over but no sign of the tin tool box of treasure.

"Maybe someone took it home for safe keeping," Merle said.

"Rotten Lowlanders," I said.

We looked around Empty Lot for clues.

"Quiet," Merle whispered. "Over here," he said grabbing me by the shirt and dragging me over closer to Old Man Hunter's land.

The waning moon illuminated little, even so we took cover in a clump of trees. "Look," Merle whispered pointing at a figure in the shadows. I could see someone messing around Old Man Hunter's shed. Old Man Hunter wouldn't need to sneak around his own farm so we decided to take a closer look. The shadow took a crowbar to Hunter's shed and popped off the latch. The figure disappeared inside the shed. Merle grabbed me by the shirt and we moved closer to the shed and hid by some rusty farm equipment.

The figured exited the shed as I peeked around the tractor tire to get a better look. My giggle reflex started and I let out a slight snicker.

This shadow heard the noise and stopped in his tracks. I

peered around the corner and saw approaching for a closer look. I slid under the tractor and took cover in some tumble weeds lodged underneath. Merle slid around the other side of the crate just as the shadow made his way around the front of the tractor. From my vantage I could only see his feet. He stopped by the tractor step and stood there as he tried to make sense of the situation. Time slowed down as I waited for him to leave. I bit down hard on my lip as I fought back the giggle. He started to bend down for a closer look. "Who the hell is out there?" I heard Hunter yell from the house. The shadow popped back up.

The shadow took cover behind the opposite side of the same old crate as Merle. I could hear footsteps coming towards us.

This fool had left everything a right mess and found himself on the wrong side of this curmudgeon who like a dog with a bone he never gave up his chew toy. He took a quick look in the shed and saw the mess. He let out a few old man curses and started investigating. I didn't want get blamed for this but I remained trapped under the tractor with Old Man Hunter on one side and the prowler on the other.

As Hunter approached the shadow panicked and ran off. Merle decided to make sure the shadow created enough of a diversion for us to escape. He grabbed several rocks and threw them in the direction of the departing figure. The first on making contact with the shadow and made a soft 'thud' sound. The others struck the trees. The sounds caught Old Man Hunter's attention and he took off in the same direction. Once Hunter had passed, I slid out from under the tractor and crawled on my belly toward the ditch where I met up with Merle. We crawled thru the ditch away from Old Man Hunters land and back into Empty Lot.

HELL IN A HAND-BASKET

"Hell in a hand-basket," Old Man Hunter complained as we drove past the shuttered farms and idle land, dry earth and tumble weeds. "That's where this country is headed," he continued gritting his teeth as he looked on.

We headed next town over to the newfangled supermarket. First of its kind in our area. My father offered to take Old Man Hunter to pick up some locks and hardware to help him repair his shed. Now the old grump had a captive audience, complaining to my father but not the intended audience of his temperance lecture as he glanced back at me from time to time mid-rant. My old man fancied himself as the modern Cowboy. A lean western type character who sported a bushy black mustache and curly hair from an ill-advised home perm my mother talked him into for reason that doesn't make sense outside of the zeitgeist. He wore worn pointy tip cowboy boots with a leisure suit and on occasion rounded out the ensemble with a dull silver bolo tie adorned with a turquoise stone in the center. Time would not be kind to this look.

"People today, they expect everything to be easy, everything pre-made from the market," Old Man Hunter continued. "Things were different back in my day, during the depression, why I never had a piece of candy until my 16th birthday," he said, looking out the window and speaking in a sort of stream of consciences. "People don't know what it's like now, to go without."

Old Man Hunter started to calm down as we drove thru Main street. He looked over at the *going out of business* sale signs in the windows and got worked up again. "Everyone wants new fancy. Back in my day, you dance with who brought you. Where's the loyalty. These cheap products from overseas, driving good people out of business. It ain't right I tell you."

"You have a point," my old man said. "Society is falling apart. Things haven't been the same since Kennedy. A couple weeks ago I heard someone fooling about in our carport."

"Yeah?" Old Man Hunter asked.

"I just opened the door and pumped my shotgun. That's an unmistakable sound. Everyone knows what that sounds is. They just scrambled off as fast as they could. That's all it took. I doubt they'll be back."

Old Man Hunter calmed down until he caught his first glimpse of the new store. Banners and streamers adorned the building announcing the pomp of the grand opening. "Pride before the fall," he said.

We went inside and got our first look at modern. The store seemed to go on forever. Cash registers in the front and aisles of merchandise as far as the eye could see. Old Man Hunter approached a long-haired stock-boy. "Hardware?" he barked.

"Right this way sir," he said acting as a tour guide leading us toward the opposite end of the store. "This is the largest store in the state," he said proudly. "Open 24 hours. Each aisle contains more merchandise than our very first store." Old Man Hunter just glanced at him, grimaced a bit and nodded. "In fact," he continued, "see this aisle here…. it's just for candy. An entire aisle for candy, can you imagine."

"We'll find it," my father interrupted before Old Man Hunter snapped.

Hunter looked around the hardware aisle at some hammers and padlocks while my father headed over to the vacuum tube tester. He had three tubes in his pocket he pulled out of our old TV. "It's one of these," he said me plugging in the first one.

He cycled thru the tubes until he found the bad one. He looked around the shelves and found a little box. He pulled it off of the shelf, opened it and compared it to the bad one. "Yep," he said. "This is the one. Now, while we are here, you can pick out something if you want."

"Anything?" I asked.

"Sure, why not," he answered.

I led him over to a display with pocket knives. I pointed to the fanciest of the Swiss army variety. "Nope," he said. Next, I presented a wrist rocket. He just shook his head no. I had recently taken an interest in burning ants, so I settled on a magnifying glass. We found a good one, large and with a smaller lens inside the main lens and solid cast plastic handle.

We caught up with Old Man Hunter near the checkout stands where he decided to settle the hash of some cashier over the length of his hair.

"Ready?" My Old Man interrupted.

Hunter just grunted and we left.

We all sat in quiet reflection in the car on the way home. I opened the package and removed the magnifying glass. It had a black handle and large plastic lens. As I examined it, I noticed an inscription the handle. I squinted to make out the words. "It says here: *Made in Japan*" I said, realizing my error one nanosecond after the words exited my mouth.

"Hell in a hand-basket," Old Man Hunter resumed his rant.

Part II

BULLFIGHTING

All good things must end and so did the strike. *Lazy teachers only held out for a week* I grumped when my mother forced onto the school bus at the crack of dawn.

I took a seat and tried to check out when he interrupted me. "Say, how'd you get that scar on your head?" Question Mark asked as he sat down next to me.

"It's like you have two eyebrows on one side," he said with one eye opened and the other eye squinting from the morning sun shining through the bus window. He rarely dropped a question once asked.

A scar bisected my left eyebrow lengthwise and I had grown weary of the questions.

Years ago, long before the lowlander infestation, my grandmother's sister Helen passed away. We met early at her house before going to the church for the services. I hid against a wall in the family room and waited for my uncle to appear. He exited his room dressed in a black suit, but still drying his hair with a towel. Advantage: Me. I attacked. I opened with a classic windmill gambit, both arms spinning in front of me in a circular motion. He put one hand on my head to fend off my opening salvo. I kept swinging and added an occasional kick to keep him honest.

He shoved me away but I refused to relent. I kept swinging wildly. He tried a distraction by holding the towel open to his side, shaking it like how a bullfighter would taunt a bull. I took the bait and charged him. I ran through the towel and he moved across the room taunting me further and again I charged.

I failed to grasp the full implications of my actions when he put the towel in front of the solid marble coffee table and I fearlessly charged at full speed.

Suddenly nothing. I found peace for a moment. I became

one with the universe and time stood still. I conversed with Aunt Helen. I experienced that blissful ignorance for a few nanoseconds before reality insists itself. With a ringing sound in my head I returned to this realm.

You really do see stars after head trauma. I had hit the edge of the coffee table head on, splitting my left eyebrow lengthwise in half like Moses of old parting the Red Sea. With blood on my face and a sudden comprehension of the situation, I returned to this realm, followed by tears.

I woke to my mother comforting me. "Oh, crying only makes it hurt more don't cha know," she said as she pressed a wet washcloth against my wound. I believed her and just as I calmed, she pulled away the washcloth to get a closer gander. "Oh, I can see the bone," she said.

My mind flooded with fear. "The bone," I cried. "Do something."

"I'm gonna to take you to the *doctor* for some stitches."

"Not that," I protested understanding her idea of 'Doctor'.

We drove past the old farms as I pressed the washcloth against my wound. The cool crisp air turned the leaves to brown and orange. We turned off the main road next to a row of mailboxes and down a long dirt road. We pulled into this farm and parked next to the horse stable. Sheep, cows, horses, dogs, animals all around his home office. *Yep, this guy.* She took me there for stitches when I cut my lip open on the same coffee table.

She led me down the steps into the basement of his house into his 'office'. Not a traditional doctor's office as he kept animals in cages in there.

This old man my father compared to W.C. Fields, met us inside. "Ah yes," he said. "Put him there on the table. I don't believe in anesthesia so you're going to have to hold him down. He's a-gonna protest," as he started threading the needle thru my torn eyebrow, pausing once in a while to say "Stomp if you need a break."

A couple weeks later the stitches were removed revealing a scar now bisecting lengthwise across my eyebrow. Hair no longer grew on the scar leaving me a double decker eyebrow on my left side. And that is how I earned the name *Tri-brow*.

TALENT

Despite the invasion of new families no one could find money for new schools. The bus ride lasted an hour to get to the next town situated at the edge of hills which led to the mine. My old man described this mining town as the dumbest place in America. Union and paranoid with somewhat tainted groundwater.

After the bus ride, I made my way to the crowded classroom. I looked around the room at the positive thinking propaganda posters on the walls and self-esteem bromides mingled with fun facts about the metric system. Nothing had changed.

I felt like a caged animal as I took my seat. *This couldn't get much worse I thought.* I started to check out.

"Welcome back," the Principals voice blasted over the intercom system interrupting my train of thought. I checked out for a minute during the announcement until "The school year will be extended a week at the end of the school year to make up for time lost during the strike."
Worker and drone bees carry out specific functions in the hive. Their entire lives are dedicated to their functions and nothing else. Permanently remaining in their cast.

I suspect the strike negotiations didn't go well for the teachers because Mrs. Olsen no longer hid her distain for me. "Are your parents interested in homeschooling? Do your parents have any plans of moving?" she often asked me in front of the entire class. I therefor adapted.

For my great discovery of the first week back, I learned how to make a popping noise by putting my right pinky in the left side of my mouth, palm out and the pinky knuckle kept stiff, forcing the pinky out of my mouth making a popping sound like that of a cork from a champagne bottle. I made that sound every time she turned her back.

"Pop" and she would turn to look. The other students would also look in my direction and I would always look over at Pinky sternly, as if he were the guilty party.

"Stop," he protested.

Good stuff I thought until she walked over to the bulletin board and removed my name.

Each Monday, the name of every kid hung on bulletin board of good. There the name remained unless the student committed an infraction grievous enough to merit the removal of his name from the good board and moved to the bad board. Each Friday after lunch the do-gooders whose names remained on the board went to a reward activity. But those whose names were removed joined the bad seeds from the other classes for study hall. I had yet to attend the reward class. Relieved now that my name had been removed I could focus on mischief freely and I kept up with the popping sound.

"Back of the room," she snapped at one *pop* over the line "And keep making that sound until I say stop." She had a new move: Every time I disrupted the class, she made me go to the back of the room and continue my disruptive act until I lost interest.

Back of the room I went where I stood making a popping noise with my mouth and pinky and her believing I would eventually learn some sort of lesson. *The joke is on her, I'm not learning.*

Despite my best intentions my name rarely lasted on the board of the good past noon on Monday. I pretended it didn't bother me but secretly I longed to join the do-gooders in the reward class. Week after week the teachers sequestered the do-gooders away from the difficult rabble to later return with grand works of art; giant cookies adorned with shiny sprinkles, pine cone bird feeders smothered with peanut butter and rolled in seeds, or paper mâché masterpieces stuffed with candies.

A Lowlander in my class called Bulldog who earned his nickname because he hailed from England, made the mistake of teaching me an obscene gesture popular in his native land. "Make a fist like this," he said. "Then hit your opposite arm joint with the fist and fold your arm up and over the fist." Bulldogs had a sketchy track record at best so I tried this out on my old man. "Don't do that again," he said. *Story checked out.*

Every time Bulldog looked at me, I made the gesture. It bothered him when I did it but it made him bothered him more wondering and he watched me out of the corner of his eye. He'd get a good enough look to see me doing it would do his best to ignore. *This'll learn him for teaching me something.*

"Back of the room," Mrs. Olsen ordered. "And keep doing it until I say stop."

I performed the arm gesture until I tired from the prank. "Mrs. Olsen," a do-gooder interrupted. "He stopped doing it."

"Keep it up," Mrs. Olsen ordered, so I repeated the gesture until recesses.

Each Friday I went to detention and worked on math worksheets or read essays with a little questionnaire at the end. I got more school work done in detention working on my own than I did during any other time.

The weeks went on like this. I stood at the back of the room performing the offending acts like fart sounds with my armpit or hitting a pencil against my throat making a hollow sound, imitating the intro to *Time* from *Dark Side of the Moon.* The latter a favorite of Spock Holidays but he would have nothing to do with it at school. He just looked down and shook his head back and forth chanting his mantra *Spock, Spock, Spock,* to help him resist temptation.

TRICK RIDING

Spock lived at the top of Dead Man's hill. After Scouts I offered a ride home to Lance on my bike. "Long way home," I said presenting the idea as his own. "Sure is an easy coast on downhill," I said.

"Hey, give me a ride home," he bossed making it seem like his idea.

"Well, alright," I said "Hop on feller." He hesitated, giving it a second thought. "Yeller?" I asked.

"No," he said and got on the handlebars. "Can you see?" he asked.

"Good enough," I told him and started down the hill. I tried to slow down a bit for what I had planned but it proved challenging with the extra weight. And just as we got near the bottom of the hill, I jumped off.

The momentum of the bike kept it upright although wobbly. It careened out of control and into some empty trash cans. *Score.* I jogged over to check on him. He looked up at me with a look somewhere between shocked and betrayed. I laughed at his face. "Right there," I said pointing to my left shoulder. "Right there man."

I hadn't seen him that angry in a while. He got up on my bike and rode it home.

"Not the most perfect of plans," I explained my caper to Merle as rode on the handlebars to Lance's house to retrieve my bike. And as we approached the bottom of the hill Merle jumped off the bike and I rode into the knocked over cans. "You're right," he said. "That is funny."

THE GIANT GILDED BOOK OF CURSES

The busses dropped us off at school before the locals showed up. With time to kill, one morning Merle led me into the school's library. "Check this out," he said. The library seemed an odd choice, but Merle never disappointed.
He pulled the 'P' encyclopedia off the shelf. He thumbed thru several pages until finding the section of 'Paintings'. "Looky here," he said. "Neckeds".
"Brilliant". I looked thru the pages trying to get to the bottom of what the fuss was about until I came across a painter called *Grandma Moses. How can this be.* I read the article about how she didn't take up painting until the advanced age of 78 years on this earth. This fact, it turned out, offended our father, that someone would take so long in life before pursuing an interest. Merle interrupted me. "You got to check this out." He led me toward the back of the room to an enormous book, perched regally on a walnut stained pine podium. A book, bound in leather with gold leaf edges, adorned with golden letters pressed into the cover spelling 'DICTIONARY'.
This was unlike any dictionary I had yet seen. Larger and far fancier.
"Every word in the English language printed inside," he said tapping on the cover. "Look-it," he said flipping thru the pages until he came upon a curse. A common curse, one I had heard my old man use several times.
"Ha, that's not English," I said.
"Sure it is," he replied. "It is if it's in there."
"Even the curses Bulldog uses," I asked.
"Yup".
"Even the curses your brothers use," I asked.
I labored under the hypothesis that curses were mostly generational. My grandmother often told me: "Your generation is headed straight to hell. We never talked the way you kids talk, why, back in my day it made quite a scandal when he said 'damn'

just one time in Gone with the Wind."

If a mild word like that could cause a scandal I therefor theorize that the curses, like people, became worse over time and had to be retired and replaced with improvements. I believed all the curses my father uttered were the products of his generation. All the curses Merle's brothers used were inventions of our generation and put *us* on that road *to hell*.

Merle flipped thru the book some more and landed on a curse I had only heard his brothers use. "Whoa, this book is modern," I said, impressed by how up to date it seemed yet baffled why knowledge of this book had been kept from me.

I MIGHT HAVE GONE TOO FAR

Two extra dim locals called Lazy Eye and Mississippi Zeke, the latter believed he earned his name for having never visited Mississippi but it reality his name came from the fact that he took his time, that is he always took a few extra *mississippis* to respond. That's how nicknames worked among the townies.

They developed a theory; Mrs. Olsen, full figured, tired, and defeated, no longer felt like enforcing order. "Come here now," she would order in a stern voice and they would test the limits of her authority by refusing and slowly backing away. "Now she just gives up," They explained.

Around this time, I noticed Mrs. Olsen had a habit of leaving her keys in the lock of a cabinet at the back of the room. *How can I use this knowledge?* I mulled. Then one day fate smiled on me. Mrs. Olsen used a key from her keyring to speak with the office over the intercom system. This two-way intercom could be accessed from our room by a keyed switch at the front of the room.

I approached Lazy Eye and Zeke with my newest caper. "During lunch," I explained to my recruits, "we take the keys, access the intercom system and utter some curses."

"Wait a sec," Lazy Eye said slowly, looking directly at me with one eye, then the other, "how we gonna get away? We'll be stuck in the class room."

"Yeah, how we gonna get away?" Zeke repeated.

"I've got that worked out. Out the window." The class room had wide louvered windows hinged on top that pushed outward to open. Mrs. Olsen like to open the windows this time of year to let in the fresh air. "We just jump out the window. Fosbury flop," I explained. A move we learned in gym class earlier that year.

"Not so fast," Lazy Eye said. "What if they figure out our voices?" He asked, surprisingly intuitive for a local but then again, they had been burned before by my ideas.

"Got that figured out too. We talk like Bulldog."

It took some work but I eventually sold them on the idea, although they never heard a bad idea they didn't like. "We just try out all the new swears but with an English accent. Cake."

Game time. I vibrated during lunch in anticipation of our latest prank. For lunch they tried passing off some imitation Chung King looking casserole disaster and a Jell-O salad. I gave the casserole a pass, but damn Zeke took his time eating every bite of that food-like attempt. *Weird people eat weird food,* I thought. I grew weary of waiting so I licked my fingers and stuck them in the food. "There," I said. "Now you're finished."

He slid my tray over and started on my casserole. I cleared my throat as if hocking up a loogie and leaned over the casserole. "Fine," he relented.

Instead of going straight outside for recess we snuck back in the classroom. We found the keys in the closet lock as expected. *This is too easy.* Zeke grabbed the keys and put them into the lock for the intercom. "Talk like, *English,*" I reminded him.

He turned the key to the left and started to talk. "Mr. Kent is a pud," he said, then turned the key back to the right and we had a good giggle. Mr. Kent being the Principal of the school.

"More English," I reminded him.

"Oh yeah." He turned the key to right again and said "bloody," and turned it off again so we could have a laugh.

He turned the key again, "I say, Mr. Kent is a pussy," he said boldly with a poor attempt at a Victorian accent. But like all stupid people he got carried away and went off script. He turned the key again and yelled "I say, Mr. Kent is a bloody tit."

He then dug deep. Instead of the old school, garden variety swears, he broke out a string of new ones. The one I had only heard Merle's brother use. A word sounding close to Mr. Kent's surname.

I figured the new modern curses too modern for him to understand because what are the odds he would've read every word from the giant gilded Book of Curses, but this caper got too hot too fast. I hip checked Lazy Eye out of the way and ran toward the open window. I leaped out head first, Fosbury flop style with a good shoulder roll on terra firma. Lazy Eye followed bumping his head on the window frame on his way out. We looked back in thru the window as Zeke headed to the back of the room to return the keys where we found them.

"Just leave 'em fool," Lazy Eye said and with that he dropped the keys on the floor and jumped out the window sans shoulder roll, knocking the wind out of himself when he struck the ground.

We couldn't relax the rest of the recess. I should have known better than to work with armatures. The recess bell rang and we slowly made our way back into the class. I tried to act naturally but not too natural, like I hadn't been involved in any trouble, but I struggled with that concept so I just sat there quietly. Lazy Eye fidgeted, tapping his pencil on his desk and Zeke just checked out.

"Now class," Mrs. Olsen began, "someone... played with the intercom during lunch. If you know anything about it, you should speak up right now." I sat still just staring at the ground.

"It sounded like Bulldog," one of them said.

This is good. The plan is working. It turned out some do-gooders in the class passed by the office mid prank and heard everything.

"I don't know what you're talking about," Bulldog protested.

Then another do-gooder pointed out, "I saw him on the playground."

I didn't count on alibis.

"No," another do-gooder interjected. "I think it was Zeke," she said. "I know him. I know his voice. He tried to be all English, but he can't."

Zeke protested, "Like I know where you keep your keys."

"Idiot," Lazy Eye said and then quickly covered his mouth.

"I didn't say anything about my keys," Mrs. Olsen said her lips disappeared in her grimace as she fought to control her rage.

"Both of you, in the hall," she said. They got up, shoulders down and went out in the hall. She followed after them. I fidgeted about while they were gone for what seemed an eternity as I worked out every possible denial I could conjure. Eventually they returned, heads down and avoiding eye contact. Mrs. Olsen followed. She stood in the doorway with a foul scowl on her face. "Arthur J. Roy, I should have known you were involved. Come here, now," she said. It had been a while since she had been this angry. *You can't trust a local for anything. Slight amount of pressure and they sing like a canary with a hernia.*

"Wha', why, what did I do?" I said maintaining my innocence.

"Now! Here," she said gritting her teeth trying to hold back her rage.

"Nope," I said confidently looking around the room with for support. Nothing, I forged into new territory now and most of them just looked stunned. She started toward me and I jogged a few steps away. Usually she had enough at this point and gave up, but this not time. That rubicon had been crossed and not only did she keep charging but gained speed.

I picked up the pace but she closed in on me quickly. I ran serpentine through the rows of desks to slow her down on the turns. Her large frame impeded her ability to make sharp corners and she plowed into the desks around each bend, but we had gone too far for her to stop now. She kept charging. I looked back over my shoulder while I ran and I thought perhaps I had indeed gone too far but figured I would eventually win the stalemate as she would tire before catching me. It reminded me of playing with matches, it started out as good fun until the fire raged out of control and I panicked trying to put it out just like the case in the great brush fire of '75.

Then the wretched do-gooders got involved thus tipping the balance of the stalemate. One by one they rose up to slow me down as I weaved my way thru the maze of desks. At first, I ran too fast to be stopped, I raised my left arm, locked at the elbow and extended forward like the Heisman fellow on the trophy. I straight armed every do-gooder who dared stand in my path. But eventually they outnumbered me knocked me off my path just enough to slow me down as I ran thru them. I then tipped over chairs behind me as I ran. She hurdled over every chair and do-gooder I left in my wake and her large buttocks gyrated upon each landing like a hyperactive kid on a waterbed.

SWARM

Honeybees swarm to benefit or protect the colony.

One last lap around the horn where at the back of the class I met an impenetrable barrier of do-gooders and like the last kid in Red Rover I hit the middle collapsing the wall of do-gooders like a spider web trapping its prey. They wrapped me up and held me there long enough for Mrs. Olsen to catch me. However, at full speed she had too much momentum and lacked the agility to slow down so much inertia in such a shorty distance and like a speeding locomotive, she couldn't stop.

She plowed into me and the web of do-gooders at full speed knocking everyone to the ground like a perfect strike. She kept a tight grip on me with one hand as she struggled to get to her feet, failing to do so on the first couple of attempts but finally managed to get upright. She pulled me up by the collar and dragged me out into the hall. "Wait here," she said grinding her teeth.

So that's where the line is.

"Stay," she said like commanding a dog and returned to the classroom. That's how it usually worked. They expected us to wait in the hall until someone from the office came by to take us to the principal's office for a good talking to. Once in a while we got lucky and no one came by, but I figured it wouldn't be the case this time as I could hear her inside on the same intercom asking for someone in the office to fetch me. After a few minutes the teacher from across the hall opened the door and shoved some fat kid out of her class. I knew this kid. Another local who spent every detention with me. He wore pointy tip cowboy boots. My mothered viewed pointy tipped cowboy boots ad 'proud' and forbade us from wearing. And on cold winter days, the pointy cowboy boot crowd used to kick me on the inside ankle bone, in a sweeping motion, sidewinder style, like kicking a field goal. The *medial malleolus* it's called as I later learned from the Giant Gilded Book of Curses. A thin layer of vintage Naugahyde did not provide sufficient protection on a cold day against a sidewinder strike from pointy tip cowboy boots.

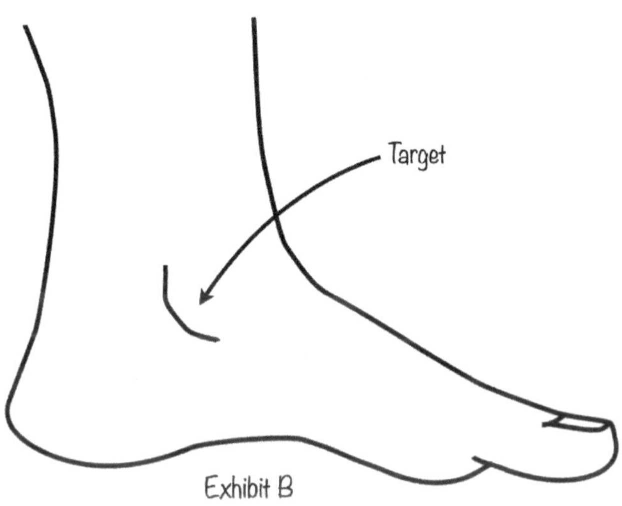

    "Watch this," the round kid said looking about and then walking over to an electrical socket. He took aim and with the pointy tip of his boots and kicked the socket. A flash of light burst forth from the socket leaving a charred flash burn on the outlet and adjacent wall.

    "Cool." I tried kicking another an outlet across the hall but I couldn't get it right with the damned square tip saddle boots. I wailed as I grew more frustrated kicking the socket harder and faster and growing more and more angry with each failure. I kicked until interrupted by the principal.

    "Tri-brow, stop that," he yelled. "What is wrong with you?"

    I could hear my mother talking before we got to the office. "I don't know why he such a bad student," she said. "At home he's always reading the encyclopedia".

    "Who taught you those words," my old man asked.

"What words?" I asked trying to maintain a semblance of deniability.

"Don't play dumb boy, how do you know what those words mean?"

"Hold on, how do I know what those words mean?" I asked. "How do you know what those words mean?"

His left eye twitched as he started to count to ten. "Who taught you these words?" he asked. "Merle's brothers?" he asked answering his own question. My father was a problem child in his day and could always sniff out mischief.

They sent me into the hall and talked it over for a while and as a condition for me remaining is school, Mrs. Olsen would each day send home a note reporting on my behavior which my parents would sign and I would return the following day.

SCOTTISH MARTIAL ARTS

I spent most afternoons after school at Merle's house learning the ways of Scottish fighting from Merle and his next older brother Chance, who earned his name because he never lost.

"Scottish Martial Arts?" Chance asked. "I can't believe you've never heard of it, you're Scottish." I looked around his room. He had a Bruce Lee poster on one wall and next it he had a small drawing of a mouse flipping off an eagle in flight about to snatch its prey. The caption read, *The Last Great Act of Defiance.* "Don't worry," he sighed shaking his head. "It's not too late."

They had a large backyard which extended to an old overgrown sycamore forest, thick with vines. There he kept a pigeon coop and pigeons as well as a couple beehives. I spent many afternoons there with his older brothers studying the wisdom of Cheech and Chong and experimenting with illegal fireworks. This is where we studied the curses of our generation, where we planned battles, adventures and shared skills and learned the fighting style of my people. This is where we observed the behavior of bees and that of the wild fowls. This is where the lessons began.

"The Scottish Arts have 33 principles. First, see this spot on your forehead," he said pointing to the top dead center of the crown of his forehead. "This is the hardest spot of your head. This is the striking plane," he explained while tapping his forehead with his knuckle to demonstrate. "Solid, Right? This is the center of your universe, the source of all your knowledge, balance and home of your soul. That's why it's so hard," he said.

Now pay attention. Anywhere else on the head isn't as hard. That's called, *the target,"* he said while pointing to other spots on his head like the eyebrow, the front of the forehead and the sides.

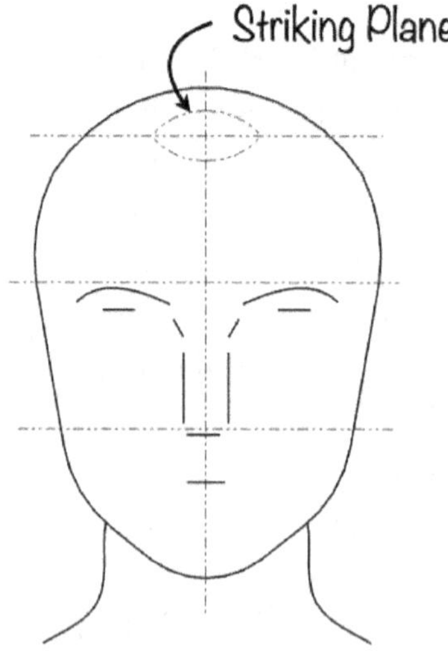

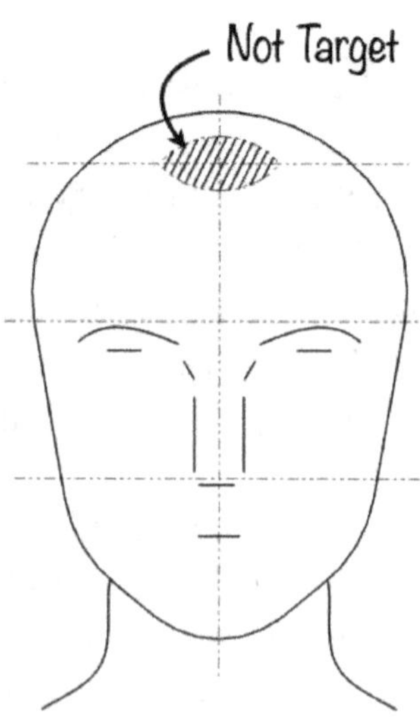

"The Target?" I asked.

"Don't interrupt. You have to learn to target these spots. It's all good, be creative and have fun with it," he said. "Allow me to demonstrate," he said quickly and then slammed the crown of his forehead into the top left side of mine.

"Dammit," I said, rubbing my head and stomping around in a circle while the pain and shock subsided. He just stood there laughing, proud of himself.

"Got it?" he asked. "Hit this board with the hard spot on your head," he ordered running me thru some practice drills. "Faster," he yelled with each blow. "Power thru the pain."

He taught me how to defend, swerve and fake, bob and weave. "Notice, when absorbing an attack," he explained, "you adjust your head just enough so your opponent misses the target and instead hits your striking plane."

"But never," he said. "Never hit hard spot on hard spot. That will eliminate your advantage."

I sparred with Merle, an expert in the Scottish Arts and followed each direct hit with a string of curses from our generation.

"If you can snatch this pebble from my hand, then it will be time," Chance said. "Ready", he asked holding out a pebble in his outstretched right hand.

"Ready," I said and reached for the pebble but he pulled his hand away too quickly.

"That'll cost ya," he said and put me on the ground and gave me a Charlie horse.

"Charlie Horses aren't Scottish. That's not part of the deal. Stop. This isn't fair," I wailed.

"There's no such thing as 'fair' in battle you sissy," he yelled.

One afternoon the taught me "The Scottish Arts are more than just combat," he said as we sat around the weeping oak tree deep in sycamore forest. there he would ask me Zen questions of the Scottish arts to help me avoid any inner peace. "How many five-year-olds do you suppose you could beat up?"

"At the same time?" I asked.

"At the same time," he answered.

I pondered the question for a spell and answered "about a hundred?"

"A hundred? You're fooling yourself."

"Not so fast," I said challenging the Master. "Are these normal five-year-olds or do they have any training in the Scottish Arts?"

"Hmm, garden variety," he answered.

I reckoned back to the great intercom prank of '76 where I met defeat by a baker's dozen of ten-year-olds and after some simple math "Ah, 26."

"Interesting," he said sitting back puffing on a sycamore barky.

Then one afternoon it happened. He challenged me to again snatch the pebble from his hand but this time I refused. "No way, you'll just beat me up some more," I said.

"How dare you defy your master," he said and put me on the ground and commenced with the Charlie horse lesson until the oldest and scariest of Merle's brothers happened by.

"Stop tormenting him already," the oldest and the scariest brother said and then put Chance on the ground. "Here, let me show you how it's really done. Make a fist with your middle knuckle extended from the rest," and then commenced to pounding on him. Chance started screaming. I had never seen him like that before. "Now that's Scottish Art."

This made me uncomfortable because I had never seen Chance lose before, but it made sense that only his older brother could defeat him. *It's funny when brothers fight though*. I thought.

JAPANESE APPLES

After the fallout of my assumed involvement in the classroom intercom prank, I received a lifetime ban from the reward class. This punishment seemed moot to me since I had never attended, in fact I always suspected a de facto ban but when I arrived at school on Monday mornings, my name had already been removed from the bulletin board of good.

Week after week, I did the math worksheets, multiplying, divisions, fractions until I had exhausted the entire supply of math worksheets. I had been in detention for so long I finished all the 4th grade math worksheets and even started on the 5th grade work and once I had finished all of those "Then go get a reading packet," Mrs. Olsen barked when I complained.

I started on the reading assignments. Articles about science, bees and plants. One, I'll never forget, having grown up around orchards. Japanese Apples. The article stated that in Japan, instead of growing many smaller apples they thin the crop by removing the smaller less desirable fruit allowing the larger apples to develop to their fullest, best tasting potential. However, here in the USA we go for quantity over quality. All the apples had an equal chance to be the best damnit, but the report hinted that the best apples were being held back by the lesser apples.

I took solace for all times I took apples from Old Man Fisher's orchard just to throw at lowlanders. *Turns out I did him a favor. His trees must therefore produce the best tasting of all apples. Thanks to me he's still in business.*

I kept quiet now not wanting to risk further wrath. I renounced my comedy and even used the *Spock Holiday* chant when needed to resist temptation.

Then one Friday morning it happened: A hush fell over the room. All the do-gooders turned to me and stared. Mrs. Olsen took pity on me. She took my name from out of her desk and replaced it on the bulletin board of good, permitting me, for the first time ever to attend the rewards class and with the following caveat: "Don't make me regret this."

"Everyone, take a seat on the floor," Miss Rose said.

All of the desks had been cleared from the center of the room and shoved closely together along the walls.

I could barely suffer the excitement. Finally, I could get my hands on some crafts, hopefully something in the dessert genre but mostly I longed for a creative outlet. Spock Holliday and Pinky sat together on the floor. I shoved my way between them and sat down ignoring how uncomfortable it made them.

Miss Rose, a slender beauty and favorite of the do-good crowd. Her long black hair flowed all the down her back and her cool garb reflected the era. Hip, a little crunchy, and not yet defeated by reality. Her classes were vibrant, energetic, creative.

"Have I got a treat for you," Miss Rose said reaching behind the desk and producing a guitar. "We are going to have a sing-a-long".

"Whoa, what the hell is this?" I asked.

"Shush," Spock said.

She put the guitar strap around her head and immediately started strumming and singing *I'm leaving on a jet plane*. I felt an anger growing. *I behaved for this.* I knew this song. My parents listened to that folky drivel. She walked around through the kids singing and strumming and focusing in on one student at a time, making direct eye contact while she sang.

This can't be happening. I sat there too stunned to react. *Where is my giant cookie, my peanut butter bird feeder, my paper-mâché masterpiece?*

"Everyone sings along," she said and commenced to play *Joy to the World*.

What is with hippies and that song?

"Now time for boola-boola" she said. Some do-gooders let out a gasp of joy. "Who wants to be it?" she asked.

They all raised their hands.

"What the hell is this?" I asked.

Spock just ignored.

She finally chose a kid and sent him out into the hallway.

She picked up a ping-pong ball off her desk and hid it on a book on the shelf at the back of the room.

"Send him in," she said and with that a kid opened the door to let him in.

He entered the room and looked around as she strummed lightly on the guitar, the rest of the class softly singing *boola-boola*.

"What the hell?" I asked in vain as Spock and Pinky refused to engage me.

The guitar playing and singing got louder when he wandered toward the back of the room. The song faded again as he meandered away from the bookshelf. He took a few steps backwards and the volume increased as he closed in on the ping-pong ball and with each baby step he took, he scanned over the area. The singing grew increasing louder and with each boola-boola I felt my temperature rise. *Life truly isn't fair.*

He snatched the ping-pong ball off the book and a cheer from the participating audience. *Finally, this nightmare can end and onto to the treats* I told myself.

"Who's next?" She asked thus driving another nail into my optimism.

A couple more laps around the boola-boola tree and then she announced "Now it's time for a *round*, the girls will start and the boys will follow." Miss Rose and the girls sang *row, row, row your boat* but at the cue for the boys to sing their part only Spock sang and only for two of the first three 'rows' before abruptly stopping not wanting to be the sole boy who sang. She didn't seem happy. *She should have known better.*

"Who likes dragons?" she asked.

All the do-gooders raised their hands.

She strummed some chords on her guitar. Starting with a major chord and then into a minor.

There's a curse upon the land
Turing everything to dust
She meandered about in the song trying to make the song work. She had a captive audience to work out her own material.

"I didn't sign up for this," I said. I tried to distract Spock and Pinky by making fart noises with my hand and armpit. Spock just looked down at the ground and chanted *Spock, Spock, Spock* over and over again.

"You still do that?" I asked but he just kept chanting.

She walked about, getting close to individual students and serenading them.

You shall not find what you seek but instead a far greater treasure.
First the fire, then the flood

She got down in my face and sang

Beware the angry dragon
He's coming for you
Beware the angry dragon
He's gonna get you

She grabbed me by the shirt and shook me about playfully. She let out a roar and then moved on to the Pinky and did the same. The do-gooders laughed at the roar as she moved about and singing the chorus to others.

Then the villagers rose up
To take on the dragon

At that point she forgot the words and quickly moved on to her interpretation of Scarborough Fair. I had long checked out at this point. *How could this possibly be worse* I thought until she interrupted my train of thought… "Now, who wants to go to a medieval fair?" She asked. All the do-gooders raised their hand each trying to be the most enthusiastic. "You're in luck," she continued "we are going to have a fair. Everyone will get to dress up and everyone will get to play a part".

With this I stopped making armpit fart noises and Spock stopped chanting Spock.

"Arthur," Miss Rose said, "you can be a monk."

"Nope, not interested," My protests fell on deaf ears as she made note of her assignment and moved on. I didn't worry. *I can ignore my way out of this* I figured, like I did with the Christmas pageant and certainly no one wanted a repeat of the unfortunate square-dancing incident of '75.

She babbled some more nonsense, assigning some other roles, blacksmiths, trades and so forth while I made more armpit noises…. "Gwen," she said, "you'll be queen and finally, Lance, you will be the king."

Normally I got out of extracurricular activities I didn't want to do by ignoring it. So many of lives little annoyances could be solved by just ignoring it, trifle things like homework but this time Mrs. Olsen checkmated me by the note she sent home with me.

After school I completed my training in The Scottish Arts. I passed all the tests, endured all the challenges. The trial of 100 Charlie horses. The *whistle or lose it* test of endurance where Chance twisted my nipple and would only release it after hearing a good whistle, incorrectly called the purple-nurple in some parts. The Indian burns, the noogies, wet willies, the wedgies, also known as a 'Mervin' in these parts.

"You don't need to do this," Merle urged as we looked at the pot of boiling water on the stove. I saw this on Kung Fu so it had to be a test. Grasshopper could not leave the monastery until he lifted the boiling pots with his forearms.

I lifted the pot for one mississippi until my arms burned and I dropped the pot of hot water on myself. Good friends will always let you follow through on a bad idea.

And finally, Chance held a stone in his open palm, shut his eyes and said "now snatch the stone."

"This is stupid," I said and walked away.

"Congratulations," he said. "you passed the final test." We celebrated with some barkies and illegal fireworks.

THE RACE

"Footrace, at Old Man Fisher's orchard," Lance issued his challenge one afternoon at Spock Holiday's house.

"Busy," I said.

"Yella?"

"No. Fine," I unanswered.

Old man Fisher had trouble maintaining his orchard in his advanced years. Wild morning glory and weeds had overtaken the orchard and covered the trees. The farm equipment exposed to the elements rusted from the neglect.

Lance led us to the unexplored portion of Old Man Fisher's land.

"What about the deranged ostrich?" I asked.

"Alpaca," Spock corrected.

"He moved it, over in the alfalfa field by the house", Lance said.

Lance opened the gate led us over to the unexplored portion of the orchard for the challenge. "A foot race the full length of the orchard," he said. He fancied himself the fastest around and invented challenges designed give him the edge. Highlanders and Lowlanders gathered for the race. Merle started the race. "On your mark, get set" and he fired his pellet gun into the air whilst shouting "Go!"

I jumped off to an early lead. In my periphery I could see Lance disappearing as I pulled ahead. In my hubris I pictured my victory over the better athlete when the ground disappeared from under me. My momentum carried me across a ditch where I smacked my shins on a cement wall on the opposite side. The wild morning glory obscured the cement ditch from view making it appear as solid ground.

Lance slowly jogged over to the ditch. He looked down at me as I clutched my shins. "Right there, right there man," he said pointing to his shoulder.

MEDIEVAL FAIR

Every year the school put on some end of year celebration, something with games and food. This year that beatnik Miss Rose pushed for a medieval themed festival. She sold the school on an interactive experience over that of passive entertainment. They therefor gave assignments. I got stuck with friar. My mother made a robe from a re-purposed bathrobe, brown and with a gold rope belt tied around my waist and hung down in front. She did such a good job with it that I hated it even more.

The only bright spot is Moses looked more ridiculous than me. He played the accordion so they assigned him to a minstrel. He got conned into some sort of elf looking costume. Green pants and pointy shoes and a hand-crafted Robin Hood looking hat made from forest green craft paper. He grabbed his accordion case and tried to make it out the door before our mother found the camera. She frantically looked thru every door for it and caught us outside and made us pose for photos that we would one day regret. We made a dash for the bus. We caught up with Merle and Chance on the bus. Merle dressed as a wizard. He had on a blue robe and a pointy hat made of blue felt.

Everyone wore costume except Chance. "Why didn't you dress up?" I asked.

"I didn't feel like it," he answered while shrugging his shoulders.

"Isn't the school making you wear a costume?" I asked.

"Yeah…. I didn't want to."

"Don't your parents know you're 'sposed to?"

"Yeah, I didn't want to," he repeated to every follow-up question I had.

At school, all the kids vibrated in anticipation. Even I found myself getting swept up in the zeitgeist until I caught a good look at Lance's garb. He wore a plastic crown an adult size white shirt, slit on the sides all the way up to the sleeves with a large Red Cross screen printed on the front. *Another mark on my revenge*

     A brief stop in the homeroom class for the formality of roll call and then they released us outside. On the playground, they set up rows of canopies and tables for activities and snacks, smartly organized and decorated to reflect the theme. In the center, they put a large makeshift stage where the older kids put on a show of musical numbers and skits for the rest of the school.

     First, we gathered around the stage to watch the acts. Moses played some old minstrel tunes on the accordion while some other kids danced about with some ribbons and cast flower petals at the crowd.

     The do-gooders ran the cupcake stand. They handed out unfrosted cupcakes and the kids packed on the frosting of their choosing and topped and finished the cupcakes themselves. Inside the tent sat King Lance and Queen Gwen holding court over the cupcake tent. This is where the trouble started. My eyeball twitched a little as I watched him perform his Kingly duties.

     Cobra, dressed as a knight, still harbored ongoing resentment from when I beaned him in the temple with a rock, sneaked up from behind and shoved a red frosted cupcake adorned with cinnamon dots in my face.

     "Th-suck on that loser," he said, looking back and forth at his friends for a laugh, proud of his prank and insult. I scraped the red icing from my face. "What'cha gonna do?" he asked mockingly. "Huh? Gonna cry?" His demeanor changed from mockery to a tough guy as he moved in closer, bit his lower lip as he tried to make me flinch by throwing a couple fake haymakers, stopping short each time. He had beat me up a few times before so I knew the fake haymakers would soon connect and he'd blame me for leaning into the punch.

     I looked over at Chance and he gave me a nod. *Game on.* Cobra reared back for another haymaker and I stepped too close for him to connect with such a wide swing. I grabbed his shirt and held him tight and slammed him in the skull with the hardest part of my head. He stumbled and fell on his backside. He rubbed the target a bit and gave me a confused look. He had never seen anything like it before. Merle's brothers had talked me into doing so many foolish things that this victory came as a surprise to me.

Haymaker defeated.

Question Mark decided to join the fracas. Also dressed as a friar. He took a couple more swings but I dodged, moved in close and grabbed hold of his robe. He adapted to this new way of fighting and grabbed my robe to hold me in place. He reared back his head for the kill shot. It all seemed to be happening in slow motion as his giant angry mug got closer to mine. With just a nano-second to spare, I adjusted my head just enough altering his trajectory to slam the front part of his melon against my striking plane.

A horrible cracking sound rang out when our heads collided like two rams locking horns. He dropped to his knees as I remained unfazed by the assault. "It's like a rock," he said fighting back some tears.

Disgusted by the display, Gwen leaned over to Lance and said "He ruins everything."

Lance stood up, removed his crown and placed it on his throne. He didn't say a word as he walked over to me.

He entered into the circle of kids. I opened with a short but quick head butt and Lance quickly and instinctively adjusted his head so I hit the hard spot of his head with mine. He had a smirk on his face and I knew that *Lance too had been trained in the ways of the Scottish Arts*.

I gave a head fake, and he adjusted, again I faked and countered. He tried to position himself so his height would be to his advantage but I kept my head down never exposing the soft part to a hit. Just like Fischer and Spassky, two great minds squared off in a battle of strategy and intellect.

At this point the teachers took notice and watched the scene unfold.

Things started to heat up when Lance made a head fake, I anticipated in and this time countered with a head butt. He barely had enough time to adjust and I struck him somewhere between the crown and the left temple. Not a direct hit but I could tell it left him smarting.

Then he tried something new, sacrificing force and accuracy for speed, he swung wild and head butted as fast as he could, not taking aim, but hitting everywhere and anywhere he could. I countered best I could but I could only react and keep him from doing any real damage.

He got in a few good licks and I gave back as best I could. I could see a bruise forming on his left temple. I noticed a bit of blood dripping from my eyebrow. He had cut open my third eyebrow again.

He gambled on victory with a wild attack but spent all his energy and had nothing left. I gripped his shirt tighter in my hands and pulled him in closer. I could tell by the look on his face he knew it would soon be over. I tilted my head back for the kill, but Deus ex-machina, Principal Kent grabbed me by the back of my robe and pulled me away whilst in the motion of throwing the decisive blow thus robbing me of my victory.

"I tried to stop him," Lance protested.
I had never seen Chance look prouder as Mr. Kent drug us off the playground.

TROUBLE

I avoided eye contact with the other kids as Principal Kent tried to sweat us out with silence. I glanced about the room. This was this first good look I got at the fustigated, black and blue knots on their heads. I took some pride in my work. I caught Lance through the corner of my eye. We looked at each other for a split second. Lance let out of bit of snicker and tried to cover it up with a cough. I fought back the urge to laugh. *It can't be healthy to hold in laughter*, I thought as I sucked in my lower lip and bit down on it to fight back the giggles. My body started to shake.

"Something funny?" The Principal barked. I learned long ago to not offer any information in these situations. I sucked my lip and cheeks into my mouth, bit down harder and shook my head left to right. I squinted my eyes so that I couldn't look at him. I tried to think of something else, something sad like a dead pet or Brian's song.

I snapped back into the moment when the lecture started by listing our crimes. "You ruined the fair for your fellow students. You've given each other cuts and bruises, one kid requires stitches because of this game of yours," he said, adding extra emphasis on the word 'game' to show is disgust.

Hearing our crimes listed so made me want to laugh more. *What's wrong with me?* I wondered.

"What is wrong with you?" he asked looking in my direction. I started to hold my breath. Through the corner of my eye I could see the other boys who were biting their lips and trying not to make eye contact.

I looked over at Question Mark and he looked me in the eye for a nano-second. Long enough to catch the giggles from me. He started to laugh but tried to cover it up with a cough.

The Principal fought back his anger and then he gave us this one parting shot "You are the worst bunch of kids I've ever seen."

I've heard that so much it's lost all meaning. I let out a big

laugh and tried to cover it but couldn't.
    "Get out, get out!" he said.

Part III

THE GREAT SNAKE ROUNDUP OF '76

Merle's father dropped off Merle, Pinky, and me at the modern grocery store to meet up with the scouts for the trip to Timpanogos cave. "You're a bit early," he remarked. "Here's a dollar each. Go inside and grab some snacks for the trip," he said, then swiftly drove away in his patrol car.

We entered the store with loot in hand. "Let's choose something healthy for our hike," suggested Pinky, which made all of us burst into laughter.

We carefully examined the candy aisle, strategizing on how to make the most of our $3.00. "Check this out," exclaimed Merle, pointing at some snacks in the hippie section. "Carob. What is happening to this country?"

Suddenly, Pinky interrupted the discussion. "Look-it," he whispered, pointing at the vertical support beam in the aisle. We all turned our attention and took notice. Attached to the beam was a wired handheld intercom system.

We approached the pillar, and Merle cautiously detached the intercom from its base. He placed the handle by my mouth and kept the button pressed, ensuring silence until we were ready to go live. When he released the button, I belted out, "Mercy sakes alive, looks like we got ourselves a convoy."

Merle and Pinky joined in, harmonizing in falsetto, "Cause we got a great big convoy, rockin' through the night, yeah we got a great big convoy, ain't she a beautiful sight."

"Hey, get off that thing!" shouted an employee, interrupting our impromptu performance. But Merle, needing closure on that tune, added one last "Convoy" before returning the handle to its base.

Being the Sheriff's son, Merle managed to escape with fewer consequences than the rest of us. Nonetheless, the employee

kept a watchful eye on us as we made our selections, completed
our purchases, and exited the store.
By the time we reached the parking lot, the rest of the scout troop
had arrived.

Spock's father loaded all of us into the station wagon, and
we set off towards the cave.   Our first adventure of the summer of
'76, heeding the siren call of the lady of the mountain and making
the pilgrimage to the Timpanogos cave, located halfway up the
mountain of the same name.

Spock Holiday's father, scout master led this expedition.
The Elder Spock resembled his son, a full-size version of young
Spock. Pale, thin and square, but a good man. He had endless
patience and being the only one willing to supervise ten boys on a
trek up the side of the mountain. "Stop throwing rocks," he said in
his nasally monotone voice as we made our way around each bend.
"No shoving," he said on the straights.

The forest ranger met us at the entrance to the cave. A big
guy, stocky with a barrel chest. His big belly tested the tensile
strength of his shirt buttons and his pants' zipper gritted its teeth
lest his girth burst forth from his dated, undersized uniform. He
had a long, gray bushy beard and a friendly inviting smile. "Come
on in," he said with a wink as he unlocked the giant wooden door
to the cave.

"Legend has it," he said spinning his yarn. "The Indian
princess died lamenting the loss of her brave who never return
from battle. Yonder," he continued pointing to a giant stalactite.
Illuminated by hidden lights it glowed a pink hue. "Behold," the
ranger said "the heart of the Mountain." I saw Spock's father
crack a smile as the ranger recounted his tall tale, leaving the rest
of us underwhelmed.

"Now I'll turn out the lights so you can see how dark it
gets," he said flicking a switch. "See," he whispered. "Critters
who live in here get around by sense of feel."

I took advantage of the lights out and tapped Lance in the
back of the knee causing it to buckle and him to fall into the cave
wall.

"Dang," he moaned. The ranger switched the lights back on. Lance looked over at me. "Right there," I mouthed without making a sound as I pointed to my shoulder. "Right there man".

We made our way back to the bottom of the trail. At the ranger's station Spock's father carried on a conversation with the ranger about the best kind of pine trees for toilet paper production while the scouts were left to explore.

The river that carved this canyon ran next to the ranger station, here the river gained speed where it narrowed around some giant borders. That is where I saw it, in the rapids on a large flat rock.

"Look-it," I said to Merle pointing to a snake sunning itself on the rock. I headed over to the boulder for a closer look when Merle grabbed me by the shirt. "Hold on." He picked up a rock and threw it at the snake missing by a foot.

Brilliant. I picked up a stone, took aim and threw one getting even closer to the snake than Merle. The snake got spooked and lifted up his tail and started shaking it rattle. This is the greatest thing I have ever seen. I had seen rattlesnakes in zoos, but never in wild and never so angry and zoos generally don't allow you to torment the animals.

The other boys caught on to our project and came over to join. It annoyed me they intruded into our fun.

The more rocks we threw the angrier the snake became. Spock Holliday observed and notified the ranger. "Um sir, I don't think they should be doing that," he said. The Ranger then did the second greatest thing I witnessed that day. He came over carrying in one hand a hollow stick with a string tied in a lasso that ran through the stick and a bag in the other. "Boys will be boys," he said as he walked by. He then wrangled the snake of wrath with the business end of his contraption, lassoing it and tightening the noose by pulling the string thru the opposite side of the hollow stick.

"Ah, the old string and hollow stick trick," Merle said and thus began the Great Snake Round Up of '76.

The next morning Merle, Pinky and myself met at my

house. I fastened a full lunchbox and my BB gun to my bike and we set off for the great canal. However, after witnessing the park ranger/snake wrangler handle the fierce rattler, every kid had the same idea and we had too many Lowlanders; Question Mark, Cobra, Granola, Lance following us.

We made our way to canal road thru a hole in the fence at the back corner of Empty Lot. This paved road ran parallel to a ditch which led to the canal. Used for irrigation, the great canal ran dry certain times of the day, more so now because of the great drought of '76. Water trapped by the mountains as snow, melts and descends to the valley below during the spring and summer. The big canal slices through the parched valley below and feeds the smaller ditches the life blood the farms and orchard needed to survive. I knew a bit about the irrigation system as I been told often that would be my future career.

Merle fashioned a snake catching stick of his own, like the one the ranger had, but he doubted we would need it as he figured "we'd only find garden snakes in these parts," he reckoned.

We stopped in a shady spot along the canal. Giant trees branches grew over the canal shading it from the sun. Merle pointed to some debris, plywood, and cardboard rubbish in the ditch below. "This should be a good spot," he said.

Lance got off his bike but took his time. Showing off, trying to push Granola over and into the ditch. He always did things like that. He ruined the Great Big Foot hunt of '75 with these antics.

"After you," I said to Lance. I had been been eating asparagus for weeks now in preparation of this revenge.

"Go ahead, I insist," Lance said. I had overplayed my hand and he sensed my pee payback.

Merle shoved us both in after growing tried of the delay.

I lifted up a piece of the plywood boards to find only worms and some grubs. Lance turned over another board and a 4-foot garden snake scurried off away from us and into a hole near a trees root. Lance reacted and ran the other way, up and out of the ditch, faster than even that of the snake. Lance is afraid of snakes.

Everyone laughed but I pondered, how can I use this knowledge.

"This is stupid," Lance said and stomped off with the Lowlanders and Pinky in tow.

"Snake hunting ain't for everyone," Merle said.

Merle and I ventured on. Past the farms and orchards. Past the hippie cult commune. Past the clearly haunted house, where we found a meadow to stop for a break. A large oak tree blocked out the sun there and vines and wild grass flourished there like an oasis.

"Lookey here," Merle said, pointing to some tiny white flowers growing on the vines that covered the ground. "These are real good," he said pulling up a vine. "You gently remove the flower from the its base like so," he said gingerly separating the white flower from its green stem revealing the opening where it attached to the base. He put the base of the flower into his mouth. "Sweet," he said.

Exhibit C

I bent down, grabbed a vine and carefully removed one of the flowers like he showed me. I put the base part in my mouth and sucked out the perfumed nectar. It had a faint, sweet taste, like that of honey but also with a hint of the same taste of the fragrance of the flower. I grabbed a few more flowers.

"Dig," he said picking some little green mallow plants growing on the ground. "Cheesees, " he said. He pulled up a few from the ground, peeled back the four leaves that hid the wild fruit to reveal a small, round light green treat, roughly the size of a pencil eraser. He popped it into his mouth. I tried a few as well. They had a soft cheese like texture. Not as tasty as the honeysuckle but still a good treat.

Exhibit D

The sticky sap of the Marsh variety of the Mallow plant is used in making the delightful confectionery that bears its name.

We leaned back against a tree in the shade and feasted on the manna offered up by the land. I felt like a king.
"Check out this asshole," Merle said.
I looked up at saw Crazy Ray on a bike. He had on a backpack and another pack on the handlebars. He focused on the

road and didn't notice us.

Merle then picked up a fresh yellow dandelion. "Observe," he said. "If'n I rub this here dandelion on your arm and if'n it turns yellow there, that means you like mustard." He was a wizard with these sorts of things. Like a shaman practicing his craft he proceeded to rub the dandelion on my arm leaving a yellow mark. "It's true," I said. "I do like mustard."

He grabbed another dandelion and said "Mommy had a baby and its head popped off" and flicked the flower off the stem with his thumb.

We spotted a bee hive in the high branches of the tree and took turns throwing rocks at the bee hive.

I thought about the saying *time flies when you're having fun*. Things couldn't get much better than now. I tried to be in the moment understanding that time is fleeting and this moment would soon fade into just a memory like a brief snapshot in time. I tried in vain to hold onto this moment as long as I could as though I were holding back the tide.

He then pulled up some wild milk thistle and made a barky. Taking out a wood match from his pocket and struck it on his pant leg. I got a bit nervous every time he did this trick because of our possible involvement in the great brush fire of '74 and again in '75. He raised the lit match to light the barky when he suddenly stopped.

"There," he said squinting, pointing with one hand and dropping the lit match with the other. I looked to see a pheasant sprinting across a field toward us, flapping its wings, trying to get airborne but couldn't get but a few feet off the ground. The pheasant charged toward us until it saw us and diverted its course. Merle jumped into action and sprinted after it, over a ditch and into an alfalfa field until he cornered it against a chain link fence. He grabbed the pheasant by the neck and said "Our work here is done. Let's go".

We rode our bikes back to his house. Merle rode with the bird under his arm like carrying a football.

At his house, we headed into his backyard Merle opened

Chance's ten-foot by ten-foot pigeon coup and chased out all pigeons and chucked in the pheasant.

I went home to check in and rest a bit from the day's adventures. About an hour later Merle phoned. "Come over," he said. "You need to see this."

I ran over fast as I could as he never disappointed. "It turns out," he explained. "Wild birds can't be caged. So, it beat its own head against the coop until it died." He lowered his head and moved it about as though he grinding it against imaginary chicken wire, demonstrating how the bird perished. "I reckon he didn't want to spend the rest of his natural life in a box. Who would?" he explained showing me the bloody, featherless head of the bird. He then carried it into the house where we plucked off the rest of the feathers.

He cleaned and gutted the pheasant and grilled it over the flame of the backyard charcoal grill. As the sun set, we feasted on chips, RC cola and wild fowl while reflecting on the best day ever so far. The bird was a bit dry.

"Old Man Fisher's land," Merle said. Fresh off the success of the first pheasant hunt Merle and I developed a yearn for adventure and a taste for pheasant. "It's overgrown back there, who knows what's hiding there,"

"Right, but he talks a lot," I reminded him.

"Eh, we can handle a talkin' to," he said.

Armed with our BB guns we set out.

We caught up Old Man Fisher in his front yard. "Say sir, you mind if we hunt for pheasants on your land?" Merle asked.

Old Man Fisher took a look at our BB guns and let out a laugh of delight.

"Pheasant hunting," he said inquiring. "That sounds like a good wholesome activity for two young men such as yourself," he said. But he had an audience and a lot of wisdom to impart. "Say, aren't you the fellas who set fire to my hay?"

"No sir," Merle said.

"You know, God looks out for babies and fools, so whenever you boys get away with one of your cockamamy stunts, that's God's way of calling you stupid," he said. "Aren't you the ones who are always teasing my Alpaca?" He asked.

"Well, about that," Merle replied but Fisher cut off.

"I've learned a few things during my 76 years on this planet," He continued. I wasn't much older than you two young men when I flew in France, during the Great War". He paused for a second. "We got into some mischief then too, just like you kids, boys will be boys," he said.

2 hours later:

"You understand," Old Man Fisher professed, "one day you young men will meet a woman, and settle down, but you can't do that unless you're willing to make something of yourselves. See, if it weren't for the male sex drive, all men would be drunken fishermen," he said. "Now, off you go. Make yourselves productive. I've got work to do".

THE GREAT HOT DOG DISASTER OF '76

The 4th of July fell on a Sunday in year of our Lord Nineteen-hundred and Seventy-Six and to celebrate this, our nation's glorious 200th my mother sewed for my brother and me our very own patriotic, red, white and blue church suits. Fashioned in the leisure style of the time from a thick heavy indestructible space-age polyester. Blue pants, red jackets, white shirts contrasted with extra-wide American flag ties made from the same thick polyester. After church, time for a photo of the family in their star-spangled ensemble and later a family get together with grilled meats and potato salad. Topped off with some sparklers for the young kids.

But the real celebration would be held on the next day. The amusement park promoted the biggest all-out celebration for the ages. *This will be the best Bicentennial EVER,* I theorized. The festivities included a carload deal, one price per car regardless of the number people. Despite the family station wagon being broke down my parents remained committed to win the carload challenge.

Plan B: The Ford Pinto. To fit all of us into this state-of-the-art compact required creative, out of the box thinking and my parents had it worked out. My father in the driver's seat and my mother in the front passenger seat. Moses and I took the back seat with our sister sandwiched in the middle. This accounted for 5 people. Two more kids laid down in the hatch back and the youngest and smallest of my sisters rode shotgun on my mother's lap like an early airbag prototype.

A diaper bag stowed on the floor under my feet with a sack of warm generic soda forcing me to sit with my knees on my chest.

Once on the road we still needed to stop for gas. *I'm certain he's doing this just to make me nuts.* "Look at that, 65 cents a gallon. If gas goes one cent higher," he complained "I will stop driving. Who can afford this?"

Finally, we made it around the bend in the mountain and I

could see the white wooden roller coast in the distance. "We'd already be there if we left when I wanted to," I complained.

"You know, the original roller coaster burned down in the great salt fire of '25," my mother interrupted trying to distract me.

At the gate, the old man paid the $25 for the carload but then tried to double down on his cheapness with a coupon. "Not on carload day," the attendant said.

Barely a generation out of the Great Depression and they still obsessed over saving a buck, in this way they carried the trauma of their parents.

"No harm in trying," he said.

The test of patience did not end inside the park. "Family time," my old man said shoving me into a tiny kid boat with my younger siblings. Knees on my chest again as we floated in a circle in two inches of water at the speed of a slow walk whilst my mother took pictures. "Smile," she said. I refused.

Eventually though, the old feller took pity on Moses and me. "Listen up," he said. "You two can go do what you want, but you have to stick together and check in with me in one hour, right here in front of the Fun House.... understood?"

"Okay," we said. I would have chewed off my own foot to get away from the little kid rides.

"Okay?" He repeated with questioning inflection in his voice.

"Okaaay," Moses said bothered by this questioning
"What!"

"Okay," he replied, but in a more submissive voice.

Finally free, we headed to the great wooden roller coaster. With the old man out of sight Moses announced "We ain't gonna be doing that."

"Doing what?" I asked.

"Checking in."

I didn't want anything to do with his scheme but I figured he'd take the heat for it.

A nation built on big ideas, ordinary would not suffice for America's 200th birthday and this place went all out. Free drinks.

Free hotdogs, all the *fixins*. Free cakes, free cookies and free cotton candy. No better way to celebrate freedom than with free stuff. Just like my parents with the carload I planned for maximum.

Then we tested the new state of the art metal roller coaster followed by free hotdogs with every topping except catsup because "only commies put catsup on hotdogs" according to old man Hunter and this day shall not be dishonored.

Next, a ride on the tilt-a-whirl followed by a quick stop for some sodas and cakes. Then some other spinning attraction that punished the rider with centrifugal force. I had seen James Bond tortured on a similar device. Followed by more hotdogs. Next the Hammer and back down for some more treats and sodas. *Greatest day ever.*

My brother mostly abstained from the free treats. A few more hotdogs for me and then time for the white wooden coaster, a classic. The coaster slowly ratcheted its way to the peak. I closed my eyes and raised my arms as the coaster descended. I could smell salt in the air from the breeze blowing off of the lake as the coaster meandered thru the bends and back to the start.

We headed to The Fun House to cool down. We made our way through the hall of mirrors, thru the mazes and the obstacles to get to the center of the building where we found a room with a giant spinning disk on the floor. Once enough people joined the grand rotating disk started spinning again. I fought a good fight to hold on but eventually yielded to the centrifugal force of the wheel it launched me off the wheel and into some other kids waiting along the perimeter. And once the wheel came to a full stop again, we jumped back on and fought our way as close to the center as we could get.

It seemed but a few minutes since our curfew passed but in reality it had been a couple of hours. Our old man caught up to us at the bumper cars. It had been a while since I had last seen him this mad.

"Where were you?" He asked when Moses then decided to poke the bear with his cover story.

"Where were we?" Moses repeated looking around. "Where were you? We were there. We looked. We couldn't see you so we...."

"Ah Bull!" He said fighting back his anger. We watched as he counted to ten blinking out each number like a hostage communicating in Morse code.

"Okay smart guys," he said. "Now you have to stay with us the rest of the day. Every time I give you to an inch" he started but midway thru his lectures it happened. My head continued to spin from all the fun rides. I got a little motion sick from time to time but I usually could power through by keeping my stomach acid in balance. But I might have overdone it and in mid-rant all the free hotdogs, all the free sodas, all the free candies, cakes and ice-creams came returned. The wages of excess paid at my father feet in one giant star-spangled wave of projectile vomit. He did a quick shuffle sliding his feet back quickly and stood on the tips of his toes while leaning forward. He stopped his rant and drug me to a nearby garbage can as fast as he could where I finished emptying the contents of my perfect day.

I laid down on a bench and tried to hold still while the world continued to spin about me. My father had calmed down and tried to comfort me. "You may as well go do what you want to," he said to Moses. "We're going to be here a while," he said a bit defeated. I saw a smirk on his face as he walked away.

"I always get sick when I eat hotdogs too," he said. "Who knows what they put in those things, lips and assholes."

I spent the rest of the day by myself sleeping it off in the Pinto and I never ate another hotdog.

THE BEE DEFENSE

"Come in," Old man Hunter barked as he grumped around his house getting ready for the work day. I had been working for him ever since my alleged involvement in the great intercom caper of '76.

I let myself in and waited in the living room. Not knowing what to do with myself I just looked around the room. On one wall above the fireplace mantel hung a triangle box with a smartly folded American flag inside. Next to the flag were some pictures of a young man. One of the young men posing in full military garb.

Old man Hunter came into the room noticed me studying the pictures. His demeanor changed and he remained quiet for a spell as though waiting for me to ask about it but I didn't really know what to say. I knew he lived alone but I never knew anything about the family who are now gone. There are times when human being can read minds and in that moment of total comprehension, I began to understand something beyond my world.

After the awkward pause he finally spoke softly, "let's get started." We headed outside.

"First, we need to do something about these ants," he said. He grabbed a shovel and dug into an ant hill and removed a shovel full of earth full of pissed off ants. He walked over to another ant hill and dumped the shovel full of ants onto the hill. He took the shovel and mixed the ants up and the existing ants immediately attacked the invading shovel ants. He then took some ants from the second pile back to the first pile where they too fought it out.

"You can trim back these vines," he told me handing me some pruning shears.

"Do you have some gloves so my hands won't get scratched up?" I asked.

"Gloves? How 'bout a pair of nylon stockings too, ya big Nancy?"

"So, no gloves?" I asked looking for clarification.

I cleared the bush away from a corner of his land near Empty Lot. There Lance and Cobra caught me on my own. "Now you're a-gonna pay," Cobra lisped, looking for payback from the last day of school.

Old Man Hunter passed by so I looked over at him for some of guidance. This grumpy old man scares everyone. *He'd know what to do.*

"Stand up for yourself ya little pussy," he shouted and walked off in disgust.

They backed me up against the shrubs. I looked around for an escape when I noticed a bee pollinating a flower on the shrubs and I flashed back to my Scottish Martial Arts training. Merle's brother taught me how to catch bees in my hands. "Cup your hands like this," holding his hands a couple inches apart with the palms arched. "Now, find a bee hovering around a flower and quickly close your hands trapping him in the hollow of both halves of your hands. The trick," he explained, "is to shake your hands together so fast so it can't sting you. Next," he said "you find someone and throw the agitated bee in their face."

The bee attack, as far as I knew it had never been tried for defense, but these were desperate times and *it's just crazy enough to work.* I snapped back to the moment and the shrubs alive with honeybees. I quickly cupped one of those pollen suckers in my hands and shook with a furry. I felt the bee bouncing off my palms as I shook. I've been stung before but I had since then perfected the method. I got the it angry enough and threw the bewildered bee at Cobra's face. The bee bounced off an inch, regained its bearings and returned to sting Cobra on the forehead. "Hey man," he said. "I'm allergic."

Protesting makes it funnier. I grabbed another, shook it violently and threw it at Lance. The bee bounced off his chest buzzed about and stung him on the ear. I grabbed another, shook and threw. Then another and another.

They retreated back to their bikes. They looked back at me in disgust. I pointed to my shoulder and shouted, "right there man".

Cobra removed a BB gun he had fastened to handlebars and took aim. His face stared to swell and his breathing labored as he took aim.

This kid always has to escalate things I thought. "Hold on, that's against the Geneva convention," I complained as I tried to run away. He just smiled a crazy grin and opened fire.

Gunned down in the back, they continued to fire until they were out of ammo. They both pointed to their shoulders and mouthed, "right there man".

BATTLE OF DEAD MAN'S HILL

We stood at the top of Dead Man's Hill, the gateway to the River-bottoms and more recently the site of the great go-cart pileup of '74. I personally had endured many humiliations on this hill on a skateboard versus random pebbles.

The Lowlanders outnumbered us that day. At least four to one. I counted those who stood against us; Skunk-boy, Porky, Tea Pot, Fig, kids who generally didn't get involved in adventures declared themselves loyal to the Lowlander cause and perhaps if it not for the great nickname project we might not be so outnumbered. All the regulars were there too, Lance, Question Mark, except Cobra who stayed home recovering from a slight allergic reaction.

Spock Holliday waited on the sidewalk, observing but refusing to take part in any war games like sort of nerdy Switzerland.

A hot dry wind blew from the west as we stared down the Lowlanders. The longer the standoff on the hill lasted the more kids showed up for the Lowland cause. Until finally Merle spoke: "Our cause is righteous. We have the high ground." And with a sniff of confidence he led the charge with the bike cavalry in tow. The Lowlanders scattered but then regrouped and surrounded the bike cavalry.

The Highland infantry caught up on foot, carrying sticks and engaged in battle with the wall of Lowlanders. Swinging their sticks gingerly at first until all order broke down and out of control until…. "Car!" Spock shouted from the sidewalk. We all stopped in our tracks and looked. At the top of Dead Man's hill a car approached. The Lowlanders went to one side of the road while the Highlanders went to the opposite to wait for the car to pass. Old man Smith passed by in his jalopy and gave us a crusty stare down as he went by.

With the car out of sight Spock shouted "clear" and the battle resumed.

Finally, I saw my opportunity. I took my BB gun from off the handlebars, pumped, took aim on Lance and fired. I compensated for the slight left pull and looked over at Spock for confirmation of a hit. He shook his head 'no'.

I pumped again and took aim but this time a Lowland bike cavalry hit me in the side. They immediately surrounded me and pulled me from my bike. With defeat in sight, the Highlanders one by one defected back home until "Car," Spock again shouted from the side of the road. Old Lady Gardener backing her new giant yellow Cadillac from the driveway but backed up too far, up over the curb and hit the fire plug across from their driveway. The fire hydrant snapped off like Merle with a dandelion top. Pressurized water lifted the back end off the ground as water shot out from underneath all sides of the car. Both sides stopped the battle and ran over for a closer look.

We watched in amazement as the water shot through the air. The water showered down on us, cooling us down until the water pressure exhausted its contents upon the parched road. The water flowed downhill past the brown lawns and into a storm drain.

The fire department and police showed up quickly for a good look around followed by some workers who dug up the base of the hydrant.

By then Old Man Gatherer returned and wandered over to investigate the commotion. Old men and young boys always took a keen interest in constructions sits, asking questions, giving advice. "You kids out here, always spreading a mess around from hell to breakfast," Old Man Young said to us shaking his boney finger.

The battle of dead man's hill ended in stalemate after great fire hydrant incident of '76, we all retreated to the highland to regroup.

The next morning Merle gathered together all those who had bikes. He collected broomsticks, dowels, sticks and with duct tape he fastened them to the bikes so the stick stuck out of the front of the bike a foot. "Now," he said, "when you get one in your sights ram 'em."

"Um, I think someone is going to get hurt," Spock complained in a whiny voice.

"Yep," Merle said.

Spock phoned the Lowlanders to meet us at Dead Man's hill. On Merle's command the Calvary peddled downhill has fast as they could and when the Lowlanders saw Merle's invention coming their way they scattered, retreating halfway back to Empty Lot.

"Keep charging," Merle ordered and we pursued them until they made a stand in front of Gwen's house. The Lowlanders then abandoned their bikes and mounted a stick-based attack.

Merle removed the joust from his bike fashioned from 6-foot bristle type broom. Holding it in both hands, equal lengths sticking out from his sides, ran into a crowd of kids doing battle, knocking them all down including a few who were on our side. He then turned around and made another pass to get a few more and any of those foolish enough to get right back up.

"You idiots are going to seriously hurt someone." Gwen's babysitter shouted from the balcony. "Someone is going to lose an eye," she said. Everyone stopped for a spell, considered the prophetic words of that crazy old witch and then resumed the fight.

We pushed them back to Empty Lot and on the cusp of victory but a crowd of adults formed at the water gate near Empty Lot.

OLD MAN HUNTER'S LAST STAND

It had been a while since I had seen Old Man Hunter so angry. He cursed at the hippie cult some old man curses while Old Man Fisher tried his best to calm him down. "Let's talk about this," Fisher said.

This hippie cult took the absolute worst elements of the failed hippie movement and organized religion and combined it into one delightful self-righteous package. The cult had been buying up some of failing farms in the lowlands and the water rights that granted to those lands.

Normally Old Man Hunter listened to Fisher, but not this time "Nuts," he said uttering an old man curse.

"Now, there's no need for that kind of language," Fisher replied.

"I won't last the summer," Old Man Hunter decried as he grabbed the wheel of the irrigation gate and started turning. "This ain't right."

A couple hippies grabbed hold of the wheel and tried to turn the wheel the opposite direction. "We have a court order," the leader insisted waving some paper about while his minions fought with Hunter. Old Man Hunter's old man strength proved too much for the hippies and he succeeded in closing the gate sending the water back to his farm.

More hippies grabbed the wheel and tried to turn the wheel back. Old Man Hunter slapped their hands away and then punched their forearms.

"Cool, Old Man Hunter's gonna beat up some hippies," Merle said.

Old Man Fisher tried to get between Hunter and the hippies to defuse the situation but being much older than even Hunter they easily pushed him aside and he fell to the ground.

The hippies fought hard trying to turn the wheel but were no match for Hunter's rage until the hippie smell became too much for him to bear and he let go. Hunter grabbed the one closest to him by the ear and kicked him in the seat of his pants and shoved him away. He grabbed the wheel again and turned it back shut.

I started to understand. My old man told me about back in the day when farmers bought and sold water shares like a commodity in these parts, and in times of droughts families when to war over these rights.

Merle's father then pulled up in his sheriff's car and both sides immediately pled their case to him.

Merle's father studied the paperwork and said "I'm sorry Hunter". And with that the hippies turned the gate and the water flowed away from Hunter's land and toward the commune.

Defeated, Old Man Hunter walked alone back to his farm.

Although Hunter's stand proved futile, it inspired us to make a stand of our own. We planned an early morning BB raid on Empty Lot. But we had to delay the attack until later that morning. "I told you guys to be ready at dawn," Merle scolded.

"I can't get up that early," Pinky wined.

We rode are the long way to Empty Lot and ditched our bikes behind some trees at Old Man Hunter's place. From his place we could see bikes there and Lowlanders moving about.

"On my signal," Merle said. "We'll open fire".

We inched closer the fort when a Lowlander spotted us. "Highlanders," he shouted and ran into the fort.

"Fire," Merle yelled and we opened fire on the fort. Our BB's hit the wood walls of the fort and bounced off doing no damage. We pumped and fired until empty.

"Come out and surrender," Merle yelled. Only silence. We took our spare BBs and started reloading when it happened. A baker's dozen of Lowland ninjas wielding flexible hot-wheel tracks exited the fort and charged us. They used the tracks like whips striking us at will in the hands and in the heads before we could finish reloading the BB guns. Pinky panicked and dropped his cache of BBs turned and ran. Two Lowland ninjas chased him down beating him in the back with their tracks. I loaded my BB gun with a handful of BBs. I pumped and fired hitting a ninja in the chest. I tried to pump again but he cracked me in the hand with his track.

Merle took held is BB gun by the barrel and swung to keep the Lowlanders at bay.

"Retreat," he yelled but the Highland army and already abandoned us. We ran toward our bikes with the hot-wheel track ninjas behind us. Once we got to our bikes Merle pulled out is pellet gun and opened fire.

"It's like scout camp all over again," Pinky wailed.

The ninjas turned and ran back to safety of the fort.

The next morning with further attacks on Empty Lot on hold, I put my old square tip cowboy boots and a cowboy hat and headed down to Hunter's place to work.

That morning we started in the barn. He kept some great old stuff in there. A bandolier belt hanging on a support beam caught my eye. It had a few bullets in the rings.

"Cool," I said. "Can I wear this?"

"I don't care," he muttered but then stopped me from putting it on. "Hold on; aren't you the fool who put a bullet on a rock and beat it with a hammer until it went off?"

"No," I said. "That was Pinky." *It was me.*

"Rubbish," he said. Not his first choice of words but suspicious of my response. "Alright," he said and slid the remaining bullets from the loops on the bandolier. "There ya go," he said and handed it back it me. It lacked a little without bullets, but I still wore it with pride.

He kept an old horse in the barn. "Grab Malory by the reins," he said. We'll put him in the field."

"Can I ride him?" I asked.

"Do you know how to ride?"

"Yes," I said.

"Ha, bull," he said. "I can tell when you're lying."

How does he always know? I wondered.

He put the saddle on him and helped me up and on. He led us out to the field by the road and Malory found short alfalfa by the road and started eating. Old Man Hunter grabbed an ax and started cleaning some brush.

After a spell, a car came by and pulled off the road by the fence where we worked. It surprised me to see a car this far off the beaten path. A woman got out of the passenger side. She had big hair and tight jeans and southern drawl. "Excuse me, young man, excuse me," she said. "Are you a real cowboy?"

Old Man Hunter's head popped up from the thickets as her question had caught his attention.

I pondered for a spell. "Yes ma'am. Yes, I am," I answered.

She took out a camera and took a picture of me on the horse. "Thank you," she said and got back in the car and drove off.

"Real cowboy? "You, you dime store fraud," he said and started to laugh. "I've been doing this for over 60 years and no one has ever asked me that."

SECRET MISSION TO THE PIT

That afternoon we met in Merle's garage to plan the next move.

"We need something new. Something big," Merle said as he paced back and forth when the deliberations were interrupted by the garage door being opened from the outside.

Pinky burst in. "Ambush," he said, all soggy and distressed.

"Explain," Merle said.

He had a welt on his face.

"Who they?" Merle asked.

"The Lowlanders, tricked me."

"Explain," Merle said. Pinky moved to a chair and started to sit down. "Not there," Merle said noticing Pinky's wet clothes. "There," Merle said pointing to a wood bench. "What happened?"

"Granola phoned me, he said they had a nudie book and I could come over to check it out. So, I went over there, but instead of a nudie book....an ambush. They hid in the bushes. They attacked me with water balloons. Lance and Cobra hid on the roof with BB guns and they shot me."

"No one picks on Pinky except me," Merle said.

Merle's brother Chance came into the garage. He had a hold of the Lowlander Granola. "Tell 'em," he said. "Go on," he said again tightening his grip and lifting him off the ground.

"Okay," he replied in a whiney voice and Merle's brother loosened his hold. "It's Crazy Ray, he's gone again. He's back in the juvie I guess."

"Keep talking," Chance continued and shook him a bit to keep him focused.

"I saw him," He said. "I saw him with your tool box".

"I knew it," Merle said. "Where?"

"On canal road. He had it hid in some bushes, then he put it on his bike and rode off."

"I don't get it," Spock said. "Where is he always going? I see him on that road all the time."

"Who care." Merle said.

"But what's out there? Nothing's out there," Spock said. "So where is he going all the time?"

"The Pit", Chance said. "He has a hideout. It's in the Pit."

Merle let out a sigh. Pinky gulped. The rest of us just stared at the ground.

"I heard about his hideout," Granola said. "I hear he has a stack of nudie books, he swiped from his old man".

"Go on," I said not wanting to sound too interested as it had been a side project of ours, to get to the bottom of what the fuss was all about and rumors of Crazy Ray's book collection grew to legendary status and now we knew where to look.

The new plan: At daybreak Merle, Pinky, Granola and I would set forth for the Pit. We would raid his secret stash of contraband and return to the fort at Empty Lot as conquering heroes.

None of us had been there before so Chance made a map for our quest. Our BB guns strapped to our backs like explorers heading off into the unknown we began our quest. Pinky had a burlap bag on the handlebars of his bike his brother used for delivering newspaper. We loaded the sack with supplies, canteens, snacks, that sort of stuff.

Granola, brought along some carob snacks and trail mix.

"Carob," Merle yelled chucking the little ball of faux chocolate back at Granola.

"What," Granola wined. "It's healthy."

Named Mason, but his parents were products of the failed hippie movement and had been members of the hippie cult for a time, and despite having left the cult remained convinced that theirs was the superior way. Mason knew no better and thus earning him his name Granola.

"It tastes the same," Granola fired back.

No one thinks that," Merle said.

Pinky made sandwiches.

We followed the road to number 51 Canal Road and

stopped a spell at the house that is clearly haunted. "Odd," Spock said. "That's not how street addresses normally work in Zion."

A chain link fence surrounded the house with a fancy gate and secured with giant old-fashioned looking lock. Merle and I studied it for a minute as we had been planning to investigate the inside but never had the time with being so occupied with the Great BB Gun War.

"Let's go," Granola insisted, clearly uncomfortable at the sight of this house now owned by the commune.

A short ride past the haunted house we came upon a ranch with an electrified fence parallel to the road. "Who can hold on the longest," Merle challenged. "One, two, three," he said with his hand hovering over the live wire. And on three Everyone grabbed hold except him. We let go once we saw we had been had. It gave shock, unpleasant enough but not unbearable and gave us a good laugh.

Without saying a word, we knew what we had to do next. We backed up a few feet from the fence and had a good ol' fashioned pissing contest. "This time for both distance and accuracy," Merle said. "The closest to the electrified portion of the fence without hitting it wins." Spock abstained and shook his head and chanted his chakra as the rest of us took aim, arched our backs and let it fly. Each one watching their stream get closer to the fence.

We had our backs to the road and just when Pinky inched his way closer to win his first contest a black sedan drove by, slowing down as they drove by to get a better look at our activity. I looked back over my shoulder to see the horrified faces of an old couple. With the driver side window down, the old lady leaned over her husband and yelled "Where is your modesty? Have you no shame?"

Merle took advantage of the distraction and hip-checked Pinky a foot forward so that his stream hit the wire and instantly knocked him backward and onto the ground.

Upon seeing this move old man sped off with his wife still settling our hash as they went.

Pinky took his time getting up. "I think it's burned," he said giving himself a good look-over.

Merle smirked, "It probably is".

"It really hurts."

"Stop it," Merle said trying to catch his breath through the laughter. We all had a good laugh except Pinky and Spock, the latter just looked and the ground and chanted "Spock, Spock, Spock".

A few more clicks down the road where, according to the map we cross the Great Canal and take the dirt road to the Pit. Merle lifted his bike with one arm, up to his shoulder, descended into the canal and crossed over to the other side. The water flowed about two feet deep there. One by one, we all followed. Pinky had a difficult time on the wet loose mud on the banks of the opposite side, slipping several times on the muck until Merle pulled him out. He emerged from the canal wet covered in mud.

We all crossed the canal except Spock. He remained on his side of the canal and just watched as we crossed that Rubicon into uncharted land chanting 'Spock' as we rode out of sight.

We rode into the sun, our bikes turned up the dust on the road. We rode until we came on an oasis. A small meadow at the base of a hill with a little tree cover. We took refuge in the shade. The dry ground still offered enough mallow and wild honeysuckle flowers to weary travelers.

We snacked on trail mix, mallow, some sandwiches and finished the feast off with the sweet nectar of the desert honeysuckle. Merle made a few barkies.

After some rest and a couple swigs from the canteen we returned to the dusty road.

The sun burdened us, weighed down upon us like carrying an extra weight. It seemed hopeless until finally "Look there," Merle said pointing to a chain link fence next to an old house. "Just like the map says."

The chain-link fence ran away from the trail and parallel to the house as far back as we could see.

"It says to find a hole in the fence," Merle said looking at the map. "Just past the old house". We walked our bikes slowly along the perimeter of the property looking for the opening.

"Yep, look-it, there," Granola said being the first to spot the break in the fence.

As we approached the hole we were interrupted by a shout, "Hey you!"

We turned around to see some chunky kid with red, unkempt curly hair making him look like a troll doll. He bore a striking resemblance to the Heat Miser. He sported denim cutoff shorts, no shirt and a pair of worn cowboy boots, pointy-tip, that were at least two sizes too large.

"Git out of my yard," he ordered.

We looked at each other, stunned, not knowing what exactly to do.

The kid squinted his eyes more, let out a whoop and charged toward Pinky at full speed. He jumped in the air and soared toward him feet first hitting Pinky in the chest knocking them both to the ground in a ginger on ginger crime. The kid jumped back to his feet. Pinky whined "Oh man" stunned and writhing about on the ground.

"Map didn't say anything about that," Merle said.

The kid had a crazy look on his face. This time he took aim on Granola who stood his ground. The kid did the same maneuver with addition of a flying scissor kick which hit Granola in the hip knocking him down. The kid jumped up again and he ran, jumped and knocked Pinky down again. "Dang," he whined. I had never seen anything like it.

Then he took aim on me. I dug my heals in to hold my ground. His oversized cowboy boots hit me in the side hip and knee knocking me to the ground. I had never seen this new type of fighting despite my expertise of Scottish Martial Arts I had no response to this new kind of attack.

He turned his attention Back on Granola. Granola tried to run away while looking back over his shoulder. The kid flew through the air and hit Granola with both feet square in the back and down he went again but this time he stayed down.

He next turned his attention to Merle. He stood still for a moment. The hot summer sun beating down on them. Merle squinted into the sunlight. The kid let out a snarl and shuffled his feet in the dirt. He lowered his head and charged. Merle stood still, not moving a muscle as the kid approached. Then, with nary a nano-second to spare, Merle stepped aside, lifted his left arm to his side, straight and level with his shoulder clotheslining the kid with his forearm hitting his forehead. The kid laid on the ground for approximately 3 mississippis while he struggled to catch his breath. He drew in a deep breath before letting out a loud wail and ran into his house crying.

"Okay, let's go," Merle said.

THE PIT

We made our way thru the broken fence and once inside I got my first glimpse of the Pit.

The Pit was aptly named. Basically a giant hole in the ground. Possibly formally a lake or maybe a crater. A horseshoe shaped plateau with a near straight drop to the bottom. We stood on top the outer rim and looked down at the 30-foot drop to the bottom.

"We need to find the trail down," Merle said while studying the map. The map foretold of a trail, where the wall crumbled and made for an easier decent to valley below.

We walked along the edge of the pit looking for the trail down. "Guys," Pinky let out a cry for help. He had stepped too close to the edge and the earth gave way under his foot. He held on to his bike with his opposite hand trying to use it as leverage to pull himself back up. Granola dropped his bike and grabbed Pinky and tried to pull him up but more earth gave way and they both started sliding off the edge. Merle walked over to them, grabbed them both by an arm and just sat down using his weight to pull them both back onto solid ground.

"Can't I count on you boys for nothing," Merle lectured.

We ventured on until came upon a spot where the edge had given way and crumbled into a steep hill which led to the promise land below. However, instead of one trail, we found three, each with its own unique challenge.

The first trail offered the most generous slope but contained several large moguls in the way.

The second hill presented the steepest path but with the fewest moguls.

The third trail seemed the most treacherous as it had ruts worn into the surface and meandered about its way to the bottom.

"Map doesn't say which trail to take," Merle said.

"Doesn't say," Granola complained. "This always happens with you guys; you think you know what you're doing but…"

"Quiet," Merle ordered.

I grew restless over the argument. "Danger is my middle name," I announced reckoning action is superior to debate. The first trail clearly had to the safest bet and I started down on my bike. This trail seemed less steep than the others but I gained speed much faster than I had expected.

I hit the first mogul at full speed. I jumped into the air and came back down hard. I wobbled and started to lose control. *Brake, brake.* My instincts told me to brake and I cranked down on the brakes in vain. I shimmied uncontrolled and at full speed onto the next mogul where the front tire of the bike hit a rut and threw over the handlebars. I landed near the bottom and slid the rest of the way down with my bike in tow.

Landing on my back knocked the wind out of me. I must have hit my head because I went away for a spell. A place where time is constant instead of fluid variable, just like when I hit my head on the coffee table and then in an instant I snapped back to this world.

"Are you alright?" Pinky shouted from up top.

Embarrassed by my fall and with bruised pride more than body I lashed out. "Shut up Pinky," I shouted, trying to cover my humiliation.

"But I didn't mean......" Pinky started to protest before giving up and trailing off.

Granola, who also didn't think things through before taking action figured he had the problem solved headed down the second trail. A smoother trail which seemed safer sped him down the hill much faster than me. The steep slope hid the sudden three-foot drop at the bottom.

He launched off the jump at full speed. His front tire hit the ground hard first after the drop and the momentum carried him up and over the front tire where he landed, skidding a bit with his bike on top of him. *It's funny when it happens to someone else,* I chuckled.

Pinky studied the third trail concluding it must be correct choice, but Pinky never took risks and refused to proceed. Merle pushed on the back of his bike with his foot. He rode down the hill, gaining speed, but lost control around the bends, struck a big rock, his feet slipped off of the peddles on impact bouncing him forward onto the support bar of his bike, but still somehow managed to bring his bike to a controlled stop where he then tipped over and slid the rest of the way down the hill. He writhed about on the ground in pain and held his crotch and screamed "Rupture."

I'll never understand the nut buster bar on boy's bikes.

He took a few minutes to recover and finally made his way to his feet, dusted himself off and walked partway up the hill to retrieve his bike and walked it the rest of the way down.

Merle observed all from on high. He studied the scene like a golfer before a long putt and chose the second path. Instead of trying to slow his decent he peddled as fast as he could. He leaned back, pulled up on the handlebars as he hit the hidden drop and landed on his back tire and gently brought the front tire to the ground like landing a jumbo jet. He hit his brakes and brought his bike to a skid and a controlled stop.

"Cake," he said.

We dusted ourselves off and set off to explore the Pit.

The dry ground reminded me of the scales on a reptile. The edges of the scales curved upward and crumbled with each step.

As the ground collapsed in spots I could make out what looked to be the top of street signs. We came upon a depot or warehouse now mostly a pile or rubble. The Great mudslide of '60 entombed the lower portion of the building underground leaving only these ruins and the tops of some street signs. "Dig," Merle said pointing to a hole in the ground. We peered down, best we could. Looked like some lockers or storage room of some kind. The disintegrating bricks on the building caused me to stop and pondered the oddity modern ruins and tragically early decay in a young country then Merle announced "Look-it".

I could make out in the distance an oasis, a cluster of wild elm trees. Yet somehow even these robust plants withered from the drought.

We rode our bikes over. There were a bunch of faded

broken boxes. A clump of wild elms obscured the opening to an old partially collapsed wooden shack.

"This is it," Merle said looking at the map.

Pinky, impetuous could no longer stand the excitement became overcome by his desire to be first to gain the knowledge of what the fuss was about, ran through the opening and into hideout but he ran back out faster than he ran in slapping himself in the head, waving his arms about screaming "Bees!" He flung himself on the ground and rolled around in the dirt until the bees finally relented and he had retreated to a safe distance. In Pinky's haste of finding the hideout he failed to notice the weathered boxes were still active beehives.

"Yep, map says to look out for bees.... look out for bees," Merle said while watching Pinky roll around in the dirt. "Some crazy old fool used to keep bees here back in the day."

"What now?" I asked.

None of us came this far just to leave empty handed, yet millions of tiny, buzzing, yellow cherubs prevented us from gaining knowledge.

Merle went to work. He gathered twigs, bits of straw, leaves, thistle, and commenced to fashioning a barky. "This is no time for a barky," I protested but he just kept working until he had fashioned the grandest two fisted barky ever seen.

"Pinky, give me a shoelace," Merle ordered.

"Man," Pinky let out a whine having to give up a shoelace, but acquiesced and removed one and handed it to him. Merle wrapped it around the barky. "Put your finger here," he said pointing at the intersection of the shoelace on the barky. Granola complied and Merle finished it with a tight knot.

Like a surgeon asking for an instrument "Magnifying glass," he ordered. I handed him my magnifying glass. He looked up at the sun for a second, adjusted the angle and bringing the focal point on the lens to a tiny bright yellow dot on the business end of the barky it started to smoke and gave off a dusty stale smell. He blew on the barky a few times while keeping the light focused on it until it reached critical mass and burned on its own.

The tightly packed barky starved for oxygen smoldered and produced a thick cloud of gray smoke

Merle walked toward the entrance of the hideout and wafted the giant barky around the entrance. The agitated bees calmed and retreated to their hives.

Smoke masks 'alarm' pheromones that are released by guard bees which keeps the colony in a state of calm.

"Skills," Merle said handing the giant barky to Pinky.

Once the bees had calmed down, we entered the shack. Chinese elm trees that surrounded the structure had now overtaken the shed and pushed thru the roof of this dilapidated barn. Light shown thru missing boards in the roof.

Merle found a tarp along one side of the lair. He pulled it back revealing several wooden milk crates full of all sorts of random items; wallets, keys, forks, cups. Even a Bible. *Who steals a Bible?* A clicker remote for a TV. *Seems like I remember someone complaining about losing theirs.* A blender, one ski pole. Merle found a fancy book with words written in gold lettering which read Golden Recourse of Ancient Instructions on Life. Merle showed the book to Granola. "That was taken from the community," he said. The community being the hippy cult, but Granola never called it that.

"I've seen him," Granola explained. "In the back yard, I saw him open the back door at the neighbor's house and huck things into the orchard where he could pick them up later."

Turns out he would work his way into people's homes, ask if he could work odd jobs or whatever size up the place, but if they turned their backs on him, he would seize the opportunity to grab anything available, clickers, lunch pail, etc.

"Lookey here," Merle said, holding up the tool box where we kept all the fool's gold and the fake fool's gold.

"I knew it," Pinky said.

Dry leaves covered the ground and cracked beneath our feet with each step. We rummaged through his loot finding everything except what we had come for.

He kept a water pail near some strange plants. A wild crab apple tree struggled to grow along the perimeter next to it and only bore a foul rotten fruit as though it had been cursed. A boulder and an old tree stump on the opposite side of the lair with some wild elms made up the perimeter. Granola kicked some empty beer bottles out of his way as he rummaged about. And while we explored Pinky found something, something hidden way down inside a crevice of the boulder. He tried to fit his chubby hand into the crack, but could not fit it in far enough to reach it.

Granola tried next and thrust his arm into the crack felt around a bit and jerked his arm back out quickly to reveal his paw covered with tiny spiders. We all laughed as he panicked and shook off the spiders of his hand and arm. *He's never gonna be the same after this* I thought. Embarrassed he said "It's not funny guys." Which made us laugh more.

I then stepped up and thrust forth my long skinny arm into the fissure of the bolder and produced a rolled magazine. I held it over my head with one arm in triumph.

It had been rolled up to fit inside the stump. I unrolled it to reveal the cover. *Excalibur no. 42* the title read across the top in fancy red letters. The young woman on the cover held a towel in front of her body strategic enough to entice but still leaving the rest to the imagination.

"Oh, *Excalibur*, classy," Merle said.

Slowly I opened the magazine to the first page. Nothing there except for a table of contents. I turned to the next page. Not much there but some article about something I didn't care about. On to the next page. The others stayed silent as they surrounded me to learn the secrets of the forbidden magazine.

I kept turning one page at a time, slowly, not wanting to miss anything but only to find lame articles. "Awful lotta words for a nudie magazine," Granola commented. Pinky grew more and more impatient with each page. "Give me that," he shouted tearing the magazine from my hands showing an initiative I had never seen from him. I tried to snatch it back but, in the attempt, Pinky dropped both the magazine and giant smoldering barky on the ground. The giant barky burst into pieces on impact and the smoldering red-hot ambers once starved for oxygen now had all the atmosphere needed for total combustion. The barky exploded when it hit the ground instantly consuming the dry brush and leaves on the ground which quickly spread to the dying elms.

Smoke rapidly filled the lair. Granola tried to loot as much of the stolen booty he could carry while Pinky tried to recover the nudie book but couldn't locate it for all the smoke. Merle grabbed the toolbox and Pinky by the shirt and dragged him out of the burning hideout.

At a safe distance, we watched as the fire grew and consumed the hideout. The fire hypnotized as it enveloped the hideout. We stood watching silent in awe at the scale like watching a giant lava lamp. Even at a safe distance we could feel the heat radiating from the fire and onto our faces.

"Damnit Stinky," I said not able to take my eyes off the fire.

A feeling of catharsis swept over me as the dancing flames spoke to us. We watched as the great inferno of '76 fury devoured all dry tinder and wild elms like watching a giant hypnotic lava lamp.

Merle glared at Pinky in disgust one last time before we mounted our bikes and headed back.

THE ESCAPE

We returned to the fort at Empty Lot late afternoon. I took the toolbox of treasure from the bag on Pinky's bike "Lookey here," I shouted holding it over my head. Even though shy one nudie book still I felt like a conquering hero, proud of my accomplishment. The victory faded as Lefty emerged from the Fort.

"Lowland treachery," shocked, I turned and asked Granola, "What is he doing here? You said he'd be gone for a while."

"Eh, that's what I heard," he said.

Crazy Ray focused his wrath on me "you think you can steal from me?"

"Hold on, you stole this stuff from us" I said. Merle taught me to never offer information but, in a panic, I blurted "And the fire was an accident".

"Fire?" he shouted, "What fire? Come 'ere". He said menacingly. *Stupid people always expected you do to what they say in situations like this.*

I looked to Merle for support, *he'd know what to do.* "You better run," he said.

Crazy Ray started toward me but fell into a covered fool's gold hole left from our mining operations. At that point I figured I stood a better chance on foot I left my bike and ran.

There's a chance I might get out of this I thought as I headed to Old Man Fisher's place. A Fosbury flop over the short cow fence followed by a sprint deep into Fisher's land.

I made a B-line toward Old Man Fisher's house. I figured he wouldn't follow me so far into Old Man Fisher's land but I looked back over my shoulder as he closed in on me. He extended his arm to grab me just I jumped over the ditch. He hit the ditch full speed, his momentum carrying him over to the opposite side of the ditch where he hit his shins and groin on the wall. I headed toward Old Man Fisher's house but was cut off by his deranged Ostrich. I cut back across the farm. I looked back at Crazy Ray, figuring this time he'd quit but he looked angrier. I thought about pointing to my shoulder but I just wanted to get out of this situation. He climbed out and limped at first but he eventually reached full speed again. I started to fatigue but kept going with both Ray and the Ostrich chasing us. I cut back thru Old Man Fisher's land and jumped thru the hidden hole in his shrubs head first with a shoulder rolled on the other side.

I ran to the wood fence. I looked back as he struggled to find a way thru the shrubs. "You're making this worse," he screamed as ostrich hit him. He gave up on finding the opening and forced his way through the shrubs.

He gained on me again as I panicked trying to find the loose board in the fence but once thru, I replaced the board best I could so he wouldn't know how to get through. He saw me though and made his way past the fence far too quickly and he again closed in on me. "You're just making it worse," he yelled.

Now in Pinky's yard, *my last chance to lose him* I thought. After which, only Dead Man's Hill stood between me and the Highland. I headed toward Princess's dog house and cut across her line of death while she slept in her dog house. She woke and ran out to defend her turf. She ran my way just as Crazy Ray again closed in on me. Ray's arms stretched out before him to grab me just as the mad, inbred, deranged Doberman darted from her den. He tripped over the charging angry Doberman and became tangled in the chain with the beast. The dog quickly shifted its attention to Crazy Ray. She pounced and bit. She sank her teeth deep into his forearm and shook her head back and forth while growling. I made good time while he punched the dog to get free. *I've never seen anyone beat up a dog before.*

It had been a long day and my legs started to give out as I climbed the steep hill toward Highland. I could feel myself slowing down as reality got the best of me. Now free of Princess he sprinted up the hill toward me. I could hear his grunts and yells getting louder as he closed in on me. As a final act of desperation, I ran serpentine up the hill which only delayed the inevitable. It seemed hopeless like when I ran from the teacher.

I looked back over my shoulder as I ran. He closed in on my again so I took refuge behind a large oak tree. I kept the tree between him and me and ran the opposite direction of his charges. He finally lunged and caught me by the ankle. He lifted me up to my feet.

Caught, now I found myself in the clutches of a very dim angry teen-aged bully. He slammed me up against the oak tree and pressed me tightly against trunk. "Don't you EVER ignore me," he screamed. I noticed blood and teeth marks on this forearm, although terrified I started to laugh. "You think this is funny?" He twisted my shirt into a ball in his fists and lifted me up.

I thought back to my Scottish Martial Arts training: a poster Merle's brother had hanging in his room. An eagle descending on a field mouse who in response only showed the eagle his middle finger with a caption that read: *The Last great act of defiance. I'm not getting out unscathed of this but I didn't have to make it easy for this dullard.* I reached back over my shoulder as and grabbed my BB gun from around back and brought it forward. I fumbled a bit as I reached for the trigger.

He let go and quickly snatched the BB gun from me and threw it on the ground. He grabbed me again, pushed me back against the tree, made a fist "prepare to meet your maker." He then stopped mid-haymaker as dumb people are easily distracted. With my spine pressed against the tree I squirmed to look over to see what had caught his attention. Every kid, every Highlander, every Lowlanders, every kid we were feuding with, everyone with an insulting nickname had come to witness payment of my karmic debt at the hands of a blustering fool.

Instead, they aimed their BB guns at Crazy Ray. "Let him go," Granola mumbled like a question, not quite sure of himself.

"Beat it," he ordered but no one budged. "I said *scram*," he bossed, this time a little angrier and menacing.

Granola moved back a little but they still held their ground without saying a word.

"I said…" he yelling until interrupted by a BB to the cheek. He let out a wimpish scream and released me from his clutch.

"Who did that?" He screamed, stomped his feet and advanced toward the army of 10-year olds. "Do you know what I could do to you." And with that they all opened fire.

Instinctively he lifted his forearm to his face to protect his eyes and tried to charge at the closest kid but the kid would just retreat far enough away while the others spread out, swarmed and attacked from behind. I took refuge from the BB's behind the tree.

In his rage, he tried in vain to lash out at them but they outnumbered him and scattered enough leaving no kid vulnerable to an attack.

I knelt down and crawled over to my BB gun. I stretched out my arm to grab it but it still lay barely out of reach. He turned avoid the barrage of BB's coming his way and saw me. I crawled faster toward the BB gun. He lunged forward grabbing both me and the gun not at the BB gun. He picked me and the gun up spun me around and held me in front of him as a shield but the Lowlanders kept shooting.

And suddenly, they stopped firing. They turned their attention to the street behind me. I could hear the squeaky brakes of a car stopping behind us. The engine shut off and a door open.

I twisted about to see Merle's oldest and scariest brother emerged from the driver's side of a '73 Plymouth Duster. Followed by Chance. Merle pushed forward the seat and got out of the back seat.

The oldest and scariest brother didn't say a word as he walked toward Crazy Ray. Ray took out a cigarette and lit it with a lighter. Took a drag and blew the smoke out of his nose. The oldest got face to face with Crazy Ray. Crazy Ray refused to make eye contact but just looked the ground. He had some welts on his face started to swell from where he had been hit with BB's.

The oldest brother dotted Lefty's eye. The kids gathered around excited to be witnessing a good thrashing. "Beat it," the oldest brother yelled looking around at all the kids. This time all the kids scrambled.

GIANT MAGNET

I minced about the house trying to work off the adrenaline rush of the day's events when Merle came over. "I brought back your bike and BB gun but I need to borrow your giant magnet," he said.

"Huh, giant magnet?" I repeated, confused by the request since I expected to hear more about his brothers and Crazy Ray.

"Yeah, giant magnet," he repeated, handing me my BB gun. I ran to my room and fetched it. On returning he thanked me for the magnet and explained: "My brother knocked Lefty to the ground. As a last act of defiance, he tried to shoot him with your BB gun, but instead hit Chance in the eye. We're going to use the giant magnet to retrieve the BB."

I closed the door and turned around to see my old man standing there.

"What have you been up to? Have you been shooting people with your BB Gun?" he asked.

"No. That would be wrong," I said, but he saw thru me. He grabbed me by the back of my shirt and started swatting me on the back side as I tried to time his spanks and high step out of it.

He grabbed a chair and sat me in the corner.

THE BAPTISM GAME

Disarmed as news of Chance's eye spread thru the land and the parents confiscated all the BB guns expecting us to find another way to settle our differences robbing me of my right to shoot Lance in the back.

There was only one way to settle this now: The baptism game. Rarely used these days but we brought back for just this situation. It works like this: Find the worst body of water around. In this case, it was the ditch behind Empty Lot. Two champions are then chosen. They enter the water and engage in hand to hand combat until one completely dunks the other in the foul, disgusting water. The victor would have full control of the fort and Empty Lot.

We met at Empty Lot around 11:30 a.m. for the battle scheduled at high noon. Chance, now wearing a patch on his one eye where Lefty had shot him, took charge. Everyone looked on in silence as we all made our way over to the ditch. We met about 100 yards from the irrigation gate where Old Man Hunter had his last stand.

The water flowed deep at that time of day despite the ongoing drought. The sun felt extra cruel. The heat reflected off of the asphalt broke down the light into waves. I took off my shirt, shoes and socks. My feet burned on the road. I pretended the heat didn't bother me and like a hot coal walker I moved slowly to the dirt on the side of the road.

I worked my way slowly into the murky water. I remembered the words of my mother: *Don't play in the ditch, it's full of bacteria. That's how you get polio.* I had second thoughts about this contest but couldn't get out of it now. I slipped a little on the wet clay dirt lined the ditch as I climbed in. The depth of the water surprised me. It came up to my chest at that spot. The water felt refreshing cooled as the sun beat down on my exposed upper half.

Lance put on a show as he approached. He hopped up and

down a bit and then threw a few punches into the air like Muhammad Ali warming up before a fight.

"Listen up," Chance said taking charge. "Let's make this a fair fight. First one to completely dunk the other wins. Simple," he added. "No cheating, no biting, no Scottish fighting. Understand? Now…. start," he said moving his arm down in a chopping motion.

Lance came out of the gate aggressive. He charged at me, grabbing me by the shoulders attempting to push me left and right in order to knock me off balance. I widened my stance but this made me more unstable forward and back. He sensed this adjustment and changed his attack, pushing me backwards then pulling me forward.

Time slowed down. He grabbed me by the back of the head with his open palm and pulled me forward, pushing me down at the same time. It felt hopeless. I could hear Merle yelling in disgust from the side. I dropped to one knee and tried to knock his arm away, but he just moved it back again.

I could feel the sun bearing down on me as the trees above failed to provide shade through the sparse leaves. I slipped further down into the muck and the deeper I sank into the murky water the harder it became to mount a defense. It now seemed impossible. Time slowed to a crawl now. He had my back now in the water as I turned my face upward to keep the water out of my mouth as Lance continued to put his weight on me.

I struggled to keep upright. With my arms pushing up against the wall of the ditch I felt a root growing out of the ground. I grabbed hold and held on to this root as my only lifeline saving me from being completely dunked into the water.

He could smell victory. He had that stupid smirk on his face. Lance let off for a second only to reach back for more momentum in order to make one final push and to end this feud for good. I pulled harder on the branch trying to keep from being dunked until the branch finally broke right as he pulled back for one final push. I lifted the root from the water and flung it at him. The wet limp root landed on his shoulder and wrapped around his neck.

"Snake!" I yelled.

Startled, he reared back and exposed his back to the water frantically trying to remove the vine from his neck, but afraid to fully grasp it at the same time. I worked my way back upright and pounced on him. I put all my weight on him and with little resistance he suffered the worst humiliation as he went all the way under water.

Chance jumped in the ditch and pulled us both out of the water. Lance angrier that I had tricked him than losing issued a protest. "No fair. That's cheating. Some water got in my mouth," he complained. "That's cheating, no snakes."

By this point even the Lowlanders were laughing at him.

"Right there," I said as I pointed to my shoulder. "Right there man".

This made him even angrier.

He kicked up some dirt. "Rematch," he demanded.

"Sorry man," Chance said. "Tri-brow won".

Lance stomped about some more and then picked up a bald abandoned tire laying on the side of the road and threw it at me. I stepped aside in the nick of time and the tire plopped in the ditch and floated downstream.

We watched in wonderment as the tire floated away in the ditch into the open gate and down a subterranean tube but never emerged from the other side. And then like a toilet at a dinner party we watched in horror as the water backed up and over the gate and into the road.

The water flowed across the street began flooding Empty Lot. Kids started to panic and dispersed. Rookie mistake. I had been involved in many controversies and running just made you look guilty.

In less than thirty minutes clogged ditch saturated the Empty Lot covering it with about foot of water and when Empty Lot could hold no more the water found a new low ground and spilled over into Old Man Hunters land.

Old Man Hunter, toiling in his fields and cursing futility of his efforts when the water flowed past his feet down the smart rows of ditches he had dug for his corn, beets and whatever else old people eat.

He walked over to the Empty Lot to investigate the origin of this miracle. "Hey, you two idiots," he said. "You know anything about this?" He asked fighting back a grin and looking at my wet pants.

Merle just shrugged his shoulders.

"I see," he said not buying our answer but in too much of a hurry to take advantage of the situation than to cross examine us further.

AND ANOTHER THING

A giant blister developed on my shoulder with a few satellite blisters around it. I figured it might be a good idea to lay low for a while from the aftermath of the great baptism game lest someone ask us questions.

However, a few days later the curiosity became too strong and we ventured back to Empty Lot to investigate the status of the great watergate caper of '76.

The council of old men had gathered at the gate to kibitz about the overflowing water. Merle and waded thru the Empty Lot and over to the gate. The old men stopped talking and looked over at us for a second before returning to their conversation.

I tried to avoid Hunter because he'd put me to back to work in light of these new developments.

Members of the hippie cult showed up at gate and one tried to climb into the opening to figure out the problem but could not get in far enough to see the blockage. Merle just snickered as we watched them struggle to find the clog.

"You two," I heard Old Man Hunter yelling from his farm. "Come over here."

We went over as ordered and all he said was "Thanks".

"There's still time to plan our next caper", Merle said and pulled out the skeleton key he recovered from the tin tool box. "This opens the house that is clearly haunted," he said.